ALEJANDRO LUC
newspaper *El Cor*
stories, *The Sicili*
into English. Ale
the friendship be
Fernando Quiñon
often accompanies

Borges in Sicily

Journey with a Blind Guide

Alejandro Luque

Translated by Andrew Edwards

Armchair Traveller
at the bookHaus

Published in Great Britain in 2017 by
The Armchair Traveller at the bookHaus
70 Cadogan Place
London SW1X 9AH
www.thearmchairtraveller.com

Previously published by Almuzara as *Viaje a la Sicilia con un guia ciego*
English translation copyright © Andrew Edwards, 2017

A CIP catalogue record of this book is available from the British Library

ISBN: 978-1-909961-44-9
eISBN: 978-1-909961-45-6

Typeset in Garamond by MacGuru Ltd

Printed and bound in China by 1010 Printing International Ltd

Contents

Introduction

Departure Plan
(in the style of Bufalino)

Genre

Travel diary to the best of places without forgetting the common-place. Sunday excursion to the only Aleph approved by the professors of geography and history. Anything but a tourist guide, or rather, a compass for getting irredeemably lost. As in a proudly topsy-turvy world, for once the words illustrate the images.

Plot

Small grand tour around Sicily. A journey via tarmac, but also along the capricious toll roads of literature, music, art and memory. An itinerary dictated by an album of photos taken of Borges during his trip around the island, allowing for a variety of shortcuts and omissions.

Cast

I, THE NARRATOR: Native of the Atlantic coast of Andalucía. A writer by trade

RO: Philologist from Castile, awarded a grant to study in Messina

IVÁN: Tireless traveller, freelance reporter, polyglot, stateless

KA: Journalist from Madrid descended from Buenos Airean ancestry, incurable film fanatic, intrepid driver

EUREKA: Fiat Punto hire car

FERDINANDO SCIANNA: Photographer from the Magnum Agency, native of the Sicilian town of Bagheria. Protégé of Leonardo Sciascia. Skilled eye and off-stage voice, in his role as the author of the cited snapshots

JORGE LUIS BORGES: Master singer, steadfast model and blind man, completely exempt from the responsibility of any literary crime that these pages may constitute

Structure

Circular, in the roundabout way of touring the island. Anarchic, consistent with the strict disorder that thoughts and feelings are in the habit of imposing.

Intentions

Chronicle of a Mediterranean odyssey. An effort to pay a debt of gratitude to friends, teachers and life's ups and downs. And to the land itself, surrounded as it is by water. A debt of gratitude, also, to the water. And a little bit of literary-therapy, as Pirandello said about his Six Characters in Search of an Author*: 'I have written this comedy in order to escape from a nightmare'.*

Luggage

'Take it, it's for you. A present,' said Iván, and winking at me he added: 'It's the last one they had. It's your Borges.'

'Your Borges,' I repeated, '... my Borges?'

IT WAS SEPTEMBER 2002 and I already had a certain fame among my friends, or notoriety, as a serious Borgiophile. I had spent almost the whole of the previous year locked up at home preparing a long essay on the Argentinean master. And if it's true what they say, that Borges is a case of the measles, I found myself in full feverish delirium with all the pustules bursting forth.

My diagnosis certainly matched the symptoms of a perfect dose of the Borgesian measles: insomnia, reddening of the eyes, a compulsive need to quote, bouts of idiocy, halfway between pedantry and self-absorption, misuse of terms like *fervent, fatigued* or *memorious*...* and a profound sense of knowing nothing, absolutely nothing.

This often happens with Borges. First you give in to the fascination of the sounds, that song of Hamelin his words possess, where even the most common ones acquire a new meaning in his hands, an unknown texture. Then you aspire to understand, you test out various keys and it's likely that

---

* Memorious is the usual English translation of *memorioso* taken from the Borges story *Funes El Memorioso*. It conveys the meaning of someone with a prodigious memory.

some doors will open. At this point you truly start to enjoy yourself. There are writers who overwhelm the reader; as if they were precious objects only displayed behind reinforced glass. Borges, on the contrary, makes you believe he is an attainable luxury – one you can touch and even try on. Little by little you discover that his universe, like all good literature, is an infinite game of clues that lead to other clues, of readings that refer to other readings, which invariably refer to life. Each one of his texts, it has been said *ad nauseum* – though it is no less true for that – seems to contain the promise of all the texts in the world. As you make progress with this system of Chinese boxes and secret passages, bit by bit you come to terms with the true dimensions of your task, your cruel limitations, your smallness. And yet Borges has the kindness not to humiliate you. Time and time again, he makes you believe you can take a step forward, that the grail of knowledge is within reach, much closer than you realise. You move on from reading his books to investigating the books others have written about him, the interviews, the collections of stories. Before you know it, you have become a devotee of the Argentinean, someone who compulsively acquires everything with his stamp on it.

I had fallen into that trap.

The tigers, the libraries, the mirrors, the labyrinths and the *malevos* were my diet and my pillow for months. On the few occasions that I emerged from my monastic cell to meet with friends, five minutes wouldn't pass without the conversation being peppered with my tiresome clichés: 'As Borges said …'; 'Ah, that reminds me of something that Borges …'; 'Yes, like that anecdote, when Borges …' The others looked at me slightly askance, seriously worried. And I, myself, was conscious that at any moment I had to say enough was enough: for the good of my family, for my mental health and even for poor Borges, who was compelling me to exhume him hand over fist, without any sense of the opportunity or of restraint. My devotion to the Argentinean, which I already knew, was bordering on the pathological limits of embarrassment.

With this in mind, after due gratitude, I confess that I didn't pay too much attention to Iván's ironic present: a collection of photographs, black and white portraits of – who else! – Jorge Luis Borges, nicely reproduced, bound in austere and thin red millboard. Both the photos and the introductory text, written in French (the edition was published by FNAC in France although it was based on a previous Italian one, I think by Franco Sciardelli), was signed by a certain Ferdinando Scianna, a name that meant little or nothing to me at the time.

I shelved away the little book, and it could be said that, as far as possible, I forgot about it.

Some time later, our language expert, Ro, got a grant from the European Union to further her studies in Sicily for ten months. She had hardly settled in Messina before she sent us an invitation to come and visit her. I loved Ro a great deal, I would have gone to the very ends of the earth, and I certainly wasn't willing to wait for nearly a year to see her again. However, the thought of travelling to the island didn't thrill me either. Sicily ... what could there possibly be in Sicily? As the clichés dictated, I imagined a dried up land, as boring as a lunar landscape, inhabited by macho types dressed in severe black with, perhaps, a scar across the face. Surely, the Sicilian men must be like Marlon Brando, Robert de Niro or Al Pacino – an idea that by no means disgusted our friend Ka – but the Sicilian women, what would they be like? Like the mamma in Mario Puzo's *Fortunate Pilgrim*?

I had to read, to prise open the treasure chest of the island's literature. And it turned out to be filled with incalculable riches. I started with Sicily's two brilliant Nobel laureates, Pirandello and Quasimodo; I followed with Lampedusa and di Verdura, which led me on to De Roberto and his monumental novel *The Viceroys*. I was captivated by the honest lucidity of Sciascia and the exciting verbal wealth of Bufalino; I turned to the great harbingers of modernity, Verga, Brancati and Vittorini; I came to the secret world of Consolo and the light detective fiction of Camilleri. Finally, I went over the travel books of Maupassant, Fest, Goethe, Durrell ... And although I'm a sworn enemy of guides, I have to recognise that Miguel Reyero's, published by Laertes, is well researched, erudite and full of good ideas.

Without noticing, I was adding an embryonic case of acute sicilianosis to my well-advanced fanatical borgiomania. My luggage was almost packed and I was brimming with eager curiosity.

On the eve of my departure, planned for July, I decided to dust down the little book with the red cover, hazardously confined to a corner of my library. The first images that I leafed through were dated Palermo 1984. Absent-mindedly, I assumed they were about the district of Buenos Aires with the same name. However, as I delved further, I noticed the eloquent place names of Selinunte and Bagheria.

So it seemed that amongst many other places, Borges had been to Sicily. I rushed to check the dates: indeed, the maestro had stopped over on the island whilst in transit between Buenos Aires and Tokyo. He was received with all the honours, the publishing house Novecento set up a prize for him with the gift of a golden rose, and he may have got an honorary doctorate. What is certain is that Scianna, a native of the island, immortalised him on his journey around the millennial Trinacria.*

Why, I asked myself, don't you take advantage of this coincidence and visit all of the places where Borges was photographed, like some fetishistic pilgrim? I could record all the impressions gained in my diary, and, perhaps, they would give me some answers to so much of the Borgesian enigma that still kept me awake at night. Or maybe it was only an underhand way of further cultivating my idolatrous

---

* Trinacria is the Greco-Roman name for the island of Sicily.

behaviour, of adding importance to the endless journey that following Borges through time and space entails.

With this in mind, I climbed on to the coach leaving for Madrid on the 2 July 2003. Iván and Ka were waiting for me there; they had been convinced to come with me after arduous negotiations. However, there was one emphatic condition:

'As we don't want to go to the extreme of setting fire to your library, Little Quixote, promise us this will be your goodbye to Borges. Something akin to shock treatment. And after Sicily, it's finished, promise.'

They were right: I promised. Between gritted teeth, but I promised, and I repeated my commitment a second before the loudspeakers announced that our plane was already on the runway, at a Barajas Airport swarming with trolleys, flowery shirts and blue uniforms.

Ro was at home on Via Noviziato Casazza, anticipating our arrival, and we had twelve days ahead of us to retrace, according to my itinerary, the everlasting footsteps of the maestro over the length and breadth of the island.

⌒

Tiredness. That's the most immediate impression you get from this close-up: Borges with his eyes closed.

Is he asleep? If so, it would be a siesta without peace. There is a grimace hardening his features, a tension in his face that neutralises the relaxing effect of the pose. His head, flecked with grey, searches for the lukewarm sun of Palermo. The background is an unrecognisable shadow. The light brightens the burnished skin of his scrupulously shaved face. Yes, he was well known for this, I tell myself: except in a youthful photo, where he displayed some stubble that almost seemed stuck on, Borges never appeared unshaven.

I wonder what the maestro is seeing through his closed eyelids. Perhaps he is resting from that succession of maddening yellow clots, the last remaining charitable glimmer conceded by his ageing blindness. Or maybe he is trying to

Palermo, 1984

recreate in his imagination the thousands of details he has only been able to guess at via the words of his travel companions: geography caught on the wind, streets, hills, fields, ruins, squares, shorelines ...

However, the weave of wrinkles drawn on his forehead and the edges of his eyes, redefined by the natural light, seem to suggest the desire for some respite. Not abandoning himself to sleep, no, never. Funes the Memorious once said: 'To sleep is to turn one's mind from the world'. But a truce, yes, a parenthesis: the desire to switch off, even for a moment, the imposing workings of his brain, a fatigued yet still relentless mechanism capable of handling unfathomable masses of memory and an overwhelming collection of readings, ideas and inventions. However, in this instant he only wants to abandon himself to the caresses of the aged Sicilian sun, with the photographic lens as the only witness.

I read Scianna's accompanying text. He recalls how Borges received a call from a radio journalist in the lobby of his Palermo hotel. They only asked him to answer two questions: 'What is wisdom, and what does the future hold for us?' The Argentinean hesitated for a moment and responded: 'Wisdom is something for others, it doesn't belong to me. As regards the future, I don't really know if it exists, but I'm no less sure that the present does.'

He then turned to María Kodama and said, resigned: 'I have become an automatic oracle.'

When it comes to analysing the image, and given that four eyes are better than two, I ask Iván to look at it carefully:

'What do you see?' I ask him.

'A tired Borges,' he answers.

'Tired of what?'

'Being an automatic oracle.'

Messina

T IREDNESS, I WAS SAYING: eight hours in a coach to Madrid, one hour by Metro to Barajas Airport, two by plane to Rome and one and half more to Catania ... and still a couple more hours by bus to Messina. I'm making these calculations as we fly over a thick blanket of cloud blocking the view below. A biblical breech soon opens up and the sky clears. There it is, this has to be the island. But I'm not able to see the guaranteed sight of Etna's august and reddened mouth.

Once on land, the heat and humidity give us an aggressive welcome. Due to the accents we hear around us and the passengers' general appearance, it would seem that foreign tourism in its mass form has not yet taken hold of this corner of the Mediterranean, which pleases us somewhat. In these times, when even the most distant places have been trampled down, and anyone runs the risk of bumping into a relative or neighbour in the most exotic destinations, the conceited idea of reaching a lesser-known island is an unbeatable way of starting.

Someone told us that a scandalously high percentage of luggage goes missing on the connections from Rome or Milan to the island. Luckily, ours comes down the baggage carrousel safely and on time. Ro is waiting for us outside, very happy. She greets us warmly with hugs and kisses and we load our luggage onto the coach. I can only remember fleeting images of the transfer; the sea looms large on one side and scattered holiday residences are grafted to the mountain side rather like tightrope walkers on the cliff edges.

IT's GETTING DARK when we arrive in Messina, 'the devastated Messina' of Goethe. Pretty it isn't, that would seem indisputable. A sad stream crossing a rubbish tip, a mangy stray dog camping by the puddles, dun-coloured façades of warehouses, vulcanised factories with signs devoured by rust, such are my unfavourable first impressions. But as you approach the centre of town, its Mediterranean spirit and graceful way of combining the coarse modern blocks with the sinuous lines of lower housing, at least give it a friendly air.

'Where Messina was on the violet waters among broken wires and ruins ...' wrote Salvatore Quasimodo. I suppose he was referring to the effects of the earthquakes, which the poet seemingly new first hand, but it would also well describe its current appearance. Devastated by massive quakes, few architectural testimonies remain of this port city's past splendour, favoured as it has been since its foundation by the Greeks. Plague, cholera and natural catastrophes have all savaged the place. They say a quake, as late as 1908, left a toll of 60,000 dead, added to which are the victims of allied bombings during the Second World War. It had to be reconstructed quickly and without care, leading to the rather ordinary design of its buildings and their curious positioning. Some say the objective was to minimise the eventual damage, to avoid a *domino effect* in case of a massive collapse.

In his novel *The Women of Messina*, Elio Vittorini, another of the island's writers, describes the dishevelled women of the town tirelessly moving stones and how each time one of these unfortunates falls over some rubble it turns to ashes. This place is a daughter of the apocalypse, a phoenix reborn from its own ashes.

AFTER COVERING A GOOD STRETCH of steeply sloping hills, we arrive at what will be our centre of operations for a few days. It's a nice flat, fairly roomy and cosy, with good views. Ro's flatmates have gone on holiday and left us their rooms. After unpacking the luggage and freshening up a bit, we decide to go out for a walk among the meagre urban delights of the city: the cathedral with its ostentatious gloom, the ancient edifice of the Customs House and the two graceful survivors of the big earthquakes – the Palazzo Calapaj and the Annunziata dei Catalani.

You'll find these on the itinerary at the tourist offices. However, as if stopping to look at the fire extinguishers in a museum, today we wanted to see more: a blind balcony raised in a corner, a ruined mansion worth a reprieve from the wrecking ball, the shadow of a statue spilling against a wall, a worn and crooked pavement appearing to lead nowhere … I see my friends delighting in all these tiny details in the landscape, combined with the enthusiasm of being together after so much time, this setting takes on an almost magical gloss and becomes *the moment*. We've hardly been here a few hours and I already know that Messina, such a plain city, will remain fixed in our memory as a happy place.

I DON'T KNOW if it's pertinent – thoughts are capricious and almost never get to the point – but I now remember an idea put forward by Italo Calvino, that while beauty is usually well defined, ugliness is always diffuse. And it's this scattering, I would add, the vagueness of ugliness, which in our eyes leaves the road open to redemption.

Borges, in his *Fervor de Buenos Aires,* also sang the praises of a sentimental urbanism that has nothing to do with the traditional norms:

Not the greedy streets
jostling with crowds and traffic,

but the neighbourhood where nothing is happening,
almost invisible by force of habit,
rendered eternal in the dim light of sunset ...

'Don't start getting heavy so soon,' cuts in Ka. 'It looks pretty to me.'

It's Thursday, a street full of bars is packed with youngsters coming and going. They're all dressed-up, as if they want to appear in contrast to the urban landscape. The guys looking macho, with designer clothes and slicked-back hair, greet each other with two kisses and instantly adopt the poses of Greek gods. The girls, elegant, provocative and somewhat exuberant, are heavily made-up and coiffed. No one seems like a character from *The Godfather* or one of Vittorini's sacrificed women. They could be night owls from any other city in the world. They flirt, drink and dance here just as they do anywhere else.

Whilst we ask for some *arancini* (rice croquettes) and *focaccia* in a bar, I reflect on the fact that we rarely truly love the city promised by the postcards and coffee-table books. We can only stake a claim for what we conquer with our modest footsteps, flagstone by flagstone, by force of habit or a kind of seduction, sudden or gentle, but always capricious, beyond any rationale. Someone once said that places like Venice, Florence and Rome exact admiration, that they demand their legitimate astonishment tax at every turn; cities like Messina are perhaps limited to a wink of complicity we can take or leave.

'Enough of the hot air,' Iván reprimands me. 'Messina is well worth the journey, or don't you know the saying? With views over the straits how can a city be ugly.* It serves just as well for Algeciras, and I'm sure you'd be equally brutal.'

---

* The original Spanish *Ninguna ciudad es fea mientras un estrecho se vea* refers to a play on words hinting that cities like women can be found attractive in certain situations.

It's true about the straits and, I guess, Algeciras too. Later, out on our terrace, we sigh with pleasure at the site of the illuminated Calabrian coast unfolding before us. I'm lead to believe that the three kilometres separating us from the peninsula have, for thousands of years, inspired legends full of apocalyptically swelling seas, monstrous denizens and other such curses, a frightening *finis mundi*. The self-same Odysseus owes part of his fame to the fact that he was the first to cross it unharmed. They also say certain cetaceans, easy to confuse with marine monsters, occasionally ply these waters. However, today, the spectacle has nothing to do with such superstitions.

We reckon that it wouldn't be difficult to swim across this stretch of sea, so close does the opposite shore seem. And at the same time the strait, much more than a mere current of salt water, allows us to feel free, isolated from the continent, as if floating away on a comfortable breeze.

Salina

THE ROMANS USED TO SAY how navigation was necessary. But in order to do that we first have to run.

It's mid-morning and we're quickly crossing the docks at Messina, a pronounced curve that gave the city its first name: Zancle (the sickle). We've dallied too long over breakfast, and if we don't get a move on we'll miss the *aliscafo* (hydrofoil). Luckily, the boat still hasn't set sail when we arrive, out of breath, at the ticket office. We take our seats and feel the motors start to stir the water under our feet. Immediately, the hydrofoil starts to lift and its blades cut incisions in the surface of the water like a giant sled.

We stop briefly at Reggio Calabria, on the other side of the strait, and then head towards the Aeolian Islands: the archipelago that got its name from Aeolus Hippotes, God of the Winds, who lived there surrounded by happiness and abundance. I trace my fingers over the map, and before I drift off into Homeric epics, I conjure up a scene from a Stevensonian adventure. I remember, as a child, I used to love drawing, over seas of blue wax crayon, fictitious geographies similar to this; islands shaped like breadcrumbs or skulls liberally sprinkled with the usual pirate hideouts. Winding broken lines would reach out from them and invariably end in an emphatic X, under which my imagination would bury chests heaped with treasure. I would then carefully burn the edges of the paper, painstakingly crease and age it, and the result seemed wholly authentic to me.

We now leave behind the greening skirts of Vulcano, and the far off Stromboli, like a breast cast adrift, in order to enter Lipari's Marina Larga, the self-same that Barbarossa, smelling of saltpetre and slime, once razed to the ground. And what remains of the imaginative cartographer of my boyhood succumbs to an explosion of joy.

Ka points out that, in a short space of time, we have passed through three islands laden with cinematographic significance. Rossellini's neorealist classic *Stromboli* was set on the island of the same name, with Ingrid Bergman in the starring role. A little later, in 1950, William Dieterle tried to do the same with *Volcano*, starring the pretty Anna Magnani, although with less success. Four decades later, Nanni Moretti returned to these parts in a highly original film entitled *Caro Diario* (*Dear Diary*).

I only know this last movie. Moretti circles Rome on his Vespa before boarding for Lipari. Once there, he visits a friend who is dedicating his life to studying Joyce's *Ulysses* (a very appropriate cultural reference) and to watching soap operas. From Lipari they take off on a journey around Salina, Stromboli, Panarea, Alicudi ... I don't remember too well what happened to them from one place to the next; I think they went in search of peace and quiet in order to write, isolation from the world, and in each location a series of eccentric incidents and strange personalities awaited them.

What I do remember perfectly well is the *aliscafo* they travelled around in, which was identical to ours.

WE HAD TO CHOOSE an island to spend the day on, and we arbitrarily decided upon Salina, an island about which we know precious little. Only a brief reference in *The Leopard* – by way of the protagonist, Fabrizio, Prince of Salina – where it's referred to as 'the island of the twin mountains, surrounded by a sea of white-flecked waves ...'

We're just approaching and there are the twin peaks, in

reality a product of the fusion of half a dozen volcanic cones. Seconds later, the *aliscafo* finishes off its foam-speckled embroidery by pulling in at the port of Santa Marina.

NOW ON DRY LAND, a large group of teenagers moves in front of us. They're at that silly age, all acne, incipient breasts and half-formed muscles; foreigners, holidaymakers, except perhaps for the odd local lad. Laughing, they walk along without any haste, they could even be a little bored, not realising the luxury their age allows them; the absolute lack of responsibility and holidays of unlimited length. A blessed age to draw pirate archipelagos. The road to maturity has other advantages, but seeing these kids makes me think they will never be so free and innocent again. Some producer would give good money to sign them up for a sequel to *Verano Azul.**

A little further down, a tourist office is selling postcards and various excursions. We go along for a closer look and stumble across a comic situation:

'*Quando parte il batiscafo ...?*' asks a somewhat confused guy at the ticket window, much to the astonishment of the woman behind the counter.

'*Aliscafo, signore, A-lis-ca-fo ...*' she replies.

'Thinking about it, to travel around the Aeolians in a bathyscaphe could be a glory for the senses,' comments Ro sarcastically.

'Sure, if you ignore the notoriously claustrophobic discomfort of those underwater contraptions,' laughs Ka. 'Better to keep your feet on terra firma.'

Although Salina's official drink is the heady Malvasia wine – a type of sherry influenced by the volcanic soil and much loved by the Roman patricians – the rigors of this July day draw us towards an iced *granita*, which the Sicilians have

---

* *Verano Azul* (*Blue Summer*) was a 1981 Spanish television series.

turned into something of an art form. We order four, with loads of cream, and savour them with relish before taking a bus from the port to the beach.

'To any beach!' shouts out Iván.

THE BACK ROADS OF SALINA are winding and narrow, but the dazzling views offered by each bend are ample compensation. The drivers sweat blood manoeuvring around, constantly hitting their cacophonous horns and trying not to turn over the tiny trucks encountered along the way. After having to change at Malfa, we get off at a stop called Pollara and head down towards the sea crossing over some sloping rocky terrain.

Various rusty signs forbid entry. But Ro assures us that prohibitions in Sicily, and perhaps in the rest of Italy, possess a very relative character. *Tutto é vietato*, ok; but if you're going to do it anyway, be quick and don't ask. So we reach Pollara beach, with its thin strip of blackish sand licked by a docile sea, upon which two sailing boats appear to be floating languidly.

In the blink of an eye, all the upset caused by the journey seems to fade away. There are no phones, nothing urgent, the day just promises to stretch out blissfully. An impressive crag rises before us and lends its shade until gone midday. Iván and Ka pamper each other with the shared towel. Ro and I scrutinise each other's skin like a couple of self-absorbed primates.

The sea around here has a Caribbean transparency, crisscrossed by little fishes with brown stripes that pay no attention to the proximity of humans. Iván suggests we swim to the islet rising up about a kilometre in the distance. I accept without hesitation. We start to swim away, and as the distance to shore widens, the haughty mountain behind reveals itself, luxuriant, full of green tones mirrored in the shifting clouds that part to unveil the sun.

Under the surface I can make out some shoals of fish, abundant patches of underwater vegetation, light and dark polished stones, and a series of pink weightless shapes which seem like octopuses at first, but couldn't be anything except jellyfish.

My condition as a sedentary smoker catches up with me about halfway through the swim: I fear my lungs aren't going to hold out until we reach the islet. And yet, I feel so happy submerged in these waters, so delicately enveloped by this Tyrrhenian Sea, there is nothing I want less than the certainties of terra firma. If I'd wanted to pay homage to Peter Gabriel, I would probably have started to swallow water desperately humming 'Don't give up'. Lawrence Durrell, who wrote a long-winded book inspired by his trip around Sicily, said the water here tasted of oysters and brine, or did they taste of the sea? I'm now too anxious to delight in playing the sommelier.

Then I start to think about Borges and his little-known love of the sea, that youthful verse of his which comes to mind like a voice of encouragement:

Remember Borges, your friend, who swam in you ...

And I look behind, not only to glimpse Ka and Ro like two small dots in the distance, but also to remember how much I enjoyed the sea throughout the entirety of my infancy, during the endless summers of those irretrievable years. With the passing of time, I regret having grown apart from the water, I regret having *dried out*.

I don't know how, but we reach the little island. Dozens of tiny cuts in my hands from the sharp edges of the shellfish are ample testimony. Due to the lack of a flag to plant in such rugged terrain, Iván claims the rock with an urgent murmuring stream of urine. There's nobody to criticise such scatological license. Looking around from here is enough to relax any sphincter, with the Monte dei Porri on one side, and the huge ring of erosion carved from a rocky outcrop on the other, like the eye of a Cyclops gazing out to the open sea.

We go back to the girls, lunch on some panini and doze for a while. When an arrogant and overly self-confident seagull marches up and down in front of us, we get up to return to the sea once more, this time to reach a nearby cove filled with more bathers. It has some odd looking galleries carved from the rock, a refreshment stall and Neolithic cave hybrid; probably a disused fishing settlement colonised by day-trippers.

On the way over, the sea proves rather troublesome. Ka suffers the electric whiplash of a jellyfish, which produces an instantaneous rash on her thigh. Urine, that's the immediate antidote, but who is willing to spill a little uric acid on our friend's leg? Iván has just emptied himself on the islet; Ro and I, in order to avoid the embarrassing situation, decide to walk off half-heartedly.

Luckily, jellyfish attacks must be commonplace here. Straight away, as a provisional measure, a girl sitting on a towel nearby uproots a prickly leaf and smears the juice from the aloe on to Ka's thigh. Soon after, other beachgoers offer us ammonia sticks; everyone seems to carry one in their bag.

'Every paradise,' Iván says in a serious tone, 'has its serpents.'

WE DISCOVER THAT ON SALINA, on this very beach at Pollara, the film *Il Postino* was shot. Inspired by Antonio Skármeta's novel, it tells the story of a friendship between a semi-literate postman and the prizewinning poet Pablo Neruda, who has settled in the Mediterranean living in comfortable exile. Yes, I do now remember the two protagonists walking along the edge of this shoreline, settling down to discuss the meaning of metaphors. And also the fishermen, pushing their boats on to land at dusk, with our islet – it's already ours, it always will be – standing out in the background.

'Seen from here, it all looks slightly untrue,' comments Ro.

'The postman could never pass this spot by chance, along this forgotten beach, let alone with his bicycle, and greet Neruda as if nothing had happened.'

'And much less go for a swim,' notes Ka, wincing with pain through gritted teeth.

'Enough about Neruda,' interrupts Iván, with more than a hint of sarcasm. 'We're here for Borges, have you got that? B-o-r-g-e-s ...'

I take it on the chin, but reply that there's still plenty of time left. Or at least I hope so. The sun is setting quickly and we must get going. On the return journey I keep leafing through Scianna's little red book, wondering how each scene looks now, and if I'll be able to collect them all, without exception, in my notebook.

I also think about islands; about Nanni Moretti jumping from one to the other. More than being a placid tourist, he seems to be fleeing, but we don't know what from. Something in insularity attracts and terrifies us. Perhaps the fact that everything, the sublime and the dreadful, comes from the same source: the sea – the riddle that unites as much as it separates. The Aeolian Islands are possibly an even more extreme case, given that it's a satellite archipelago, linked in turn to a large island – pure insularity squared.

Literature hasn't resisted this attraction. Thomas Moore wanted his *Utopia* to be an island; Wells questioned the limits of science on the *Island of Doctor Moreau*; Bioy Casares set *The Invention of Morel* in perversely similar territory; Defoe, and then William Golding, used the island as a metaphor for the return to the origins of civilisation; D. H. Lawrence created his parable of isolation in *The Man Who Loved Islands* ... and so the list goes on.

I don't remember Borges making much reference to these geographical phenomena, except perhaps the green islets of the Tigre Delta, but he never tired of professing his admiration for the literature of islands such as Britain, Ireland, Japan, Iceland and the Greek archipelago. For many, it seems the cultural flowering of these places is due to a pressing need to find their own identity and to reaffirm it. Seeing themselves surrounded by water, maybe human beings ask with more curiosity or anxiety who they are, and to what they belong. I don't dispute this, but it seems an insufficient explanation. The influence of a powerful linguistic tradition is, I think, also necessary, supported if possible by an imperial past. This would explain why, among other things, Java, Madagascar or, indeed, Malta haven't left a legacy that reaches the heights of their illustrious colleagues.

In Cuba, which has certainly given many good books to the world, I've clearly seen this characteristically insular equilibrium between the miraculous and the tragic. While Eliseo Diego speaks of the island being 'surrounded by God on all sides', his colleague Virgilio Piñera refers to 'the wretched circumstance of water on all sides'. Where one sees the divine, the other sees the demonic.

The recurrent fantasy of the typical continental is to take refuge on an island, whilst the islander's is to escape. There are, of course, exceptions: I once interviewed another Cuban poet, Manuel Díaz Martínez, who went into exile from the biggest of the Antilles only to show up in Cádiz, which could be considered another island, and finished up living in the Canaries. I asked him if the islander mentality was, in his case, a misfortune. 'It's always advisable to have an island in reserve', was his answer.

Although the *aliscafo* doesn't have a deck, the stern has an open passageway, and acts as a smoking area. Exhausted and happy, the four of us let ourselves be slapped around by the discordant winds as we wait for the clamorous sunset. We've never seen such a tranquil sea, hardly ruffled by the criss-crossing of the boats.

'I'm not sure ... if it wasn't in these waters that Homer chose to shipwreck Odysseus?' says Ro doubtfully.

'I'd be truly surprised if they ever had violent storms around here,' adds Ka. 'On an afternoon like this it's much easier to imagine our hero safe and sound, enjoying the view from the prow of his ship.'

There are no marine monsters or sirens in sight except for the *aliscafo* greeting the few small boats crossing our path. Without wanting to, or rather, without wanting to avoid it, I start to recite Borges, this magnificent spectacular poem:

> They say that Ulysses sated with marvels,
> Wept tears of love at the sight of his Ithaca,
> Green and humble. Art is that Ithaca
> Of green eternity, not of marvels …

I get interrupted by the voices of the crew:

'Stromboli! Stromboli!'

I can't recall with certainty anything of the disembark-ation; I retain nothing of that eternal spectacle, green and humble. I only know that in front of the dock at Scari, lit by the last light of day, I felt a wounding touch, a sweet pain in the pit of my stomach. As if a jellyfish were, silently and treacherously, swimming through my very core.

❧

Borges' hands are closed around his cane. According to a catalogue I managed to find, it's a sturdy example made from dark wood, a straight or T-handle model, especially recom-mended for users with a weak constitution or lack of stability.

In the background, slightly out of focus, the dark tie, white shirt with starched collar, the impeccable black suit with lines of four shining buttons on each wrist. A gleaming badge in the buttonhole, the pen poking out from the top pocket, although at this point Borges used to dictate rather than write … perhaps, it was a symbolic present.

The wrinkled palms are in strong contrast to the backs of the fingers, smooth, lightly shaded by hair growth. The nails, though, look long and untrimmed. I would bet that the maestro, like me, had to take his nail scissors from his toilet bag at Rome Airport.

Palermo, 1984: The hands on the cane

The image reminds me of a collective exhibition of photographs that I saw in Valladolid with Ro some time ago. It was called *La main* (the hand) and as its name indicates, it was a series of what you could call 'palm portraits'. At first, it was fun to identify celebrities by using their hands as the only clue. After a while, they became creatures without owners, authentic parts for the whole, autonomous entities invited to transcribe their message. Some were coarse, threatening, caressing, languid, gnarled, fragile, corpulent, even rigid. But never silent.

I try to hear the hands of Borges, but I suffer rather Siculan interferences. Such as this simile from Sciascia:

Hands that look more like roots ...

and, indeed, one has a tendency to confuse flesh with wood, as if the fingers were extensions of the cane's upright trunk. Or there is this from Bufalino's novel, *Blind Argus*:

Closed on the pommel of the cane the two hands of perfidious slightness ...

Or this passage from *Mastro-don Gesualdo* by Giovanni Verga,

> Look, what hands!

where the reader really believes he can picture them: large, hard, unconquered and tired. Or there is a dialogue of Vitaliano Brancati's in which the cane's role is a singular sign of life:

> You see that cane? It must be buried with me, I
> want to take it into the hereafter in case,
> on the other side, you're allowed to run into
> yourself from fifteen years ago!

Even Borges himself distracts me with the memory of his 'Milonga of Manuel Flores', which gets right to the point:

> I look at my hands in the dawning,
> I look at the veins contained there,
> I look at them in amazement
> as I would look at a stranger ...

Or there is the poem, no less appropriate, dedicated to his famous lacquer cane, with which the maestro kept up a completely unreciprocated friendship. As he would add melancholically, 'things are not aware that one exists':

> In spite of its authority and firmness, it is curiously
> light ...

Words, words, words. Nothing concrete. I listen. Nothing. I pay more attention. I light a cigarette. Silence. Come on, I ask them, tell me. Something, anything. I can't close this chapter just like that.

But they stay there, fixed to his cane, like the talons of a mythological bird perched on a branch.

'Hands of Simurgh ...' I note.

A while longer, I bend my ear closer to the paper, nothing.

At that moment, I remember the four welcoming tomes making up his *Complete Works*, the volume of his collaborative work, the books of interviews and conversations, and an endless series of titles written about him and his writing, all of which are bowing my favourite shelves. And I understand that these tired hands, the hands of Borges in the Palermo of 1984, the hands of a man who would breath his last just two years later, could only hold one message: that they had already said all they had to say.

Messina, Acireale, Agnone Bagni

B AD NEWS, GUYS. I've left my driving license in Spain.
The breakfast congeals in our mouths. Ka was our
faithful driver, the Queen of the Asphalt who, as planned,
must drive us to all corners of the island. If we need to depend
on buses and trains, we'll lose too much time at stations. Ro
and I don't even know how to drive a dodgem car. As for Iván
… well, Iván does have a license, but his infamous recklessness
seriously frightens us. Even he is startled when all our eyes
turn to him. Besides, we can't rely on him for all the ground
we have to cover.

We try to improvise a solution and split up into two
groups. Iván and I will go to the port to hire a car, while Ro
and Ka will try to file a false robbery report. If they get the
corresponding document, there will be no problem if we get
stopped by the traffic police. The car hire office isn't far from
the house, so, according to Sicilian habit (or surely that of
the entire Mediterranean, from Ceuta to Greece), we decide
to stroll the distance along the succession of slopes and steps
where Sisyphus would be in his element. After handing over
the necessary documentation and signing the required guar-
antees, the friendly guy at the Rent a Car solemnly hands
over the keys to a Fiat Punto. '*É nuova*', he assures us. We
search the parked vehicles until finding it. And there it is, not
exactly *nuova*, but certainly silver and shiny.

We phone the girls straight away and give them the good
news in a rather unorthodox Latin:

'*Habemus machina!*'

They haven't had so much luck; the suspicious *carabinieri* have put every kind of obstacle in the way of processing the report.

Iván will, therefore, be the provisional driver. We load the boot, cross ourselves and confront the motorway with the daft anxiety that quickens the heart at the start of any mini adventure. Right now we feel superior to Goethe, greater than Maupassant. We are the genuine conquerors of Trinacria, the Autonauts of the Cosmostrada.

THE SICILIAN COUNTRYSIDE is able to satisfy all tastes. Iván and I are reminded of our Lower Andalusian landscape, whereas Ro and Ka find it puts them in mind of their Old Castile. However, us southerners gain the upper hand when, from Giarre, we turn towards Riposto and follow the line of the coast. The sea, always different, is always our sea.

Iván is beginning to suffer with the island's traffic. Continual overtaking, breaking, horn blowing, onslaughts and ambiguous signals would make the most mild-mannered driver reach breaking point. The road is too narrow, the people behind the wheel too audacious. Though, by a strange mechanism of ventricular and alimentary contractions, the traffic flows. Simply and miraculously, *it flows*.

Hungry and stifled by the heat, we take a comfort break in Acireale, though nothing manages to catch my imagination; not the walk through its sun-baked streets, nor the view of the cathedral with its unfinished tower, the baroque palaces surrounding it or the panorama from the Belvedere gardens, where we'll be squeezed from the viewing point by a swarm of tourists. Everything is very clean and peaceful, but perhaps the day spent on the beach yesterday has softened our senses too much, perhaps we're expecting Sicily to possess an exoticism that doesn't correspond to reality – the fact remains we find little to see on a whirlwind stop.

By way of consolation, reading about Acireale, it seems that it shares a long seismic tradition with Messina. Greek in origin, Byzantine in its splendour, an earthquake in the twelfth century destroyed the old city of Acis leaving no stone standing. Phillip IV of Spain later added the suffix *reale*, only to sell it with total disregard a few years after. Time passed and a new tremor again flattened the place, but the locals felt so attached to it that, helped by good planning, they didn't rest until it had been raised up again. The profusion of churches in the area, so many that Acireale ended up being known as the 'City of the Hundred Bells' or the 'Vatican of the South', must be directly proportional to the need of divine protection felt by the populace. A burst of mystic Monopoly: thanks for keeping us alive, a church; protect us from the next, another church. And so on until today.

While I savour the fine, concentrated flavour of the celebrated ice creams produced here, a timely emergency extinguisher for our burning throats, a beautiful sculpture catches my eye. The figure represents the myth of Galatea, the Nereid who rejected Polyphemus for her beloved young Acis, who has in turn given his name to the town and other nearby settlements, such as Aci Trezza (setting for Giovanni Verga's *House by the Medlar Tree*) or Aci Castelo.

Unfortunately the Cyclops, bearing a grudge, didn't hesitate in flattening his rival under a rock: an early precursor to the crimes of passion that so sadly afflict the Latin world. However, the gods, to avoid being characterised as mean or lazy, made a river of clear water from his blood, enabling him to meet Galatea in the sea.

'Perhaps it's a coincidence, but take a look at this,' says Iván showing us a tourist brochure. 'Acireale, spa town. Springs with sulphuric, sodium chloridic, iodic and radioactive waters ... For dermatological, rheumatic and respiratory disorders.'

'... And according to Homer, sentimental ones too,' adds Ro.

'I wonder, can you bathe in the same lover twice?' mutters Ka, in a sarcastically Heraclitian manner.

I'm sure that all these therapeutic emanations must be due to the proximity of the volcano Mount Etna, but it's rewarding to think that we're in Galatea's backyard; the very same who inspired so many mediocre bucolic poets, but also Cervantes and Góngora.

'And did they really know Sicily, or write about it second-hand?' asks Iván.

'It seems the author of *Don Quixote* spent a long time in Messina and Palermo, while preparing for the Battle of Lepanto,' answers Ro. 'I also know he dedicated a few verses to a Sicilian poet that he'd known in prison, a certain Antonio Veneziano, or Veneziani ...'

'And Góngora?'

'He didn't make it here. Quevedo sure, he worked as a diplomat on the island. But I remember the Cordoban Góngora described the island with some resounding and convincing images, like "Bacchus' Cup" and "Pomona's Garden"':

Where the Sicilian sea its froth disgorges,
The Lilibeo's foot with silver lacing
This either is the vault of Vulcan's forges ...

The sea appears again, without any trace of Góngoresque white horses, rather like a tray of mercury on this hot morning where the air is hanging heavy. Then I look around and truly notice the harmonious dialogue between land and sea, very typical of the Mediterranean, and with a backdrop so lacking in the baroque. It's funny how grandiloquent myths prosper in settings like this, which are simple to the point of seeming like exercises in style by some upstart landscape artist.

'I suppose it's your fault, you writers,' Iván teases me. 'The plain language of Mother Nature is too simplistic for you, so you go and twist rhetorical phrases until your imaginative summaries can't see the wood for the trees.'

I don't argue. Certainly, Borges found Góngora's Polyphemus positively ugly, bordering on coarse. He even reproached him for always writing about mythologies that he, himself, didn't believe. I reckon that the maestro would have also preferred the simple landscape of Acireale to the sophisticated verbal mechanisms of Spain's Golden Age.

However, the baroque has taken root so deeply in Sicily, Andalucía and in Latin America that it runs through almost every aspect of our lives, although each area shows its own peculiarities. I once had a very interesting conversation about this with Edmundo Desnoes, another Cuban writer I greatly admire. He spoke of the historic baroque as a Christian defence against the individualism and economic rationalism that, he said in his guttural voice, 'followed the ninety-five theses that Luther nailed to the door of Wittenberg church'. While in the greater part of Europe this trend was established from positions of power, language was also changing, as with 'the sharpened diamonds of Quevedo and the slippery pearls of Góngora', according to my friend: a fortress made of epithets on the war path. 'The problem is the baroque entertains, but it doesn't reveal,' he added. 'We have won with words. But it's not enough.'

WE CONTINUE OUR JOURNEY in the direction of Syracuse, passing the spot where Polyphemus got up to his old tricks. Blinded by Odysseus, he started to throw rocks onto the boats in which the hero and his companions were fleeing, while raging at his father, Poseidon, to avenge the insult by making their journey impossible. They managed to escape safe and sound, but the projectiles hurled by the injured colossus still remain today as gigantic rocks, or at least according to popular myth.

I must confess that, since reading my first abridged version of *The Odyssey* (I belong to a generation that learned of the classics in bite-sized chunks, if not in cartoons), I felt a real compassion for this character whom I always imagined as a giant simpleton without malice, however ferociously he was painted by Homer. The fact that Odysseus tricked the Cyclops by calling himself Nobody, got him drunk and escaped from his cave before executing the rest of the crafty plan, was somewhat effecting; but driving a stake through his only eye seemed an unnecessary cruelty to me – an atrocity. The current creators of children's versions must agree with me, because the recent copies I have seen in the hands of my nephews, at the height of euphemistic omission, only refer to the hero tricking Polyphemus. Any more political correctness and the event would end up being a simple detached retina.

I'm not sure if it's a sufficient act of justice but the little boat now offering tours along the coast, as far as Catania, is known as the *Vaporetto Polifemo*. To be one-eyed in the middle of such Mediterranean richness is to lose your counterbalance; however, to be blind, to be 'deprived of the diverse world', as Borges would say, may mean something more than the loss of the landscape. With his sight gone, the poor Cyclops, floundering in the dark, may also have lost a part of his being, the real choice of recognising himself in his surroundings – something the Argentinean maestro also knew well.

HALFWAY, WE DECIDE to stop for a dip in the crystalline waters, which we'd spotted from the road, with the majestic silhouette of Etna standing out in the background.

'The volcano is also an inexhaustible fount of mythology,' I comment. 'Some say that Zeus, when fighting the Titans, threw Typhon into the centre of the earth, and that he still spits lava when he gets mad. Others say how Vulcan set up his forge here, allowing Velázquez to portray him at the point of using his hammer; and we can't forget Empedocles, who sacrificed himself by jumping into the crater, only leaving behind a pair of golden sandals that the contemptuous volcano was quick to spit out.'

'Seen from here, Etna doesn't look so fierce, but there are more than enough reasons to fear it,' warns Ro.

'If we had time, I'd love to try reaching the top,' says Ka. 'Although what I'd really like to see is the lava spilling down the sides, at night, like in the documentaries.'

'Don't give it ideas,' cuts in Iván, somewhat apprehensive. 'The quieter it is, the more attractive it is.'

With all the chat we nearly forget the beach. We go down to Agnone Bagni, which, close up, is really disappointing. The sand is covered with a wide variety of rubbish and dirt. Big jellyfish suspended on the crest of the waves advise against swimming. Despite all this, sinking my feet into such hostile terrain, mingling my footprints on the shore with Ro's leaves me feeling content until well into the night.

Everything is calm and we carry on according to plan; the Fiat Punto's wheels run along the road. And in the volcanic subsoil, no doubt, the blood of Acis, the son of the Faun, follows its course.

Syracuse

MUCH HAS BEEN WRITTEN about the similarities between our Cádiz and cities like Havana, Cartagena de Indias, Vera Cruz or San Juan in Puerto Rico. Yet there's nothing I know of regarding Syracuse, or the place that features as the jewel in the crown of my Sicilian prayer book, the part of town known as Ortygia. Much the same as here, my hometown is an island more or less linked to terra firma, both were walled to repel aggressors who came from the ocean, both have contemplated the splendour and decline of ancient civilisations. It could be due to all these coincidences, but the air, the nooks and crannies, the self-same sea, the glances from the people, all seem to welcome me with a touching familiarity.

The other half of Syracuse, actually called Terra Firma, isn't overflowing with delights. However, it's enough to cross Corso Umberto I, and pass over the bridge dividing the dock in two in order to enter Ortygia, a place of unique charm and soothing light.

We park next to the ruined Temple of Apollo, with its robust columns conquered by wall rocket, and go in search of accommodation. Nearby, hung from a balcony, a faded sign says: Hotel Philadelphia and displays a hand-painted phone number. In the doorway below there is no trace of anything, not even the classic little plaque showing the stars or keys indicating the quality of the establishment.

'What do you reckon?' asks Ro. 'Shall we try ...'

We call the number, it rings. On the other end of the line, a female voice says that she'll come down straight away.

It's less than five minutes before a pretty and amiable young lady arrives, her age is difficult to work out. She shows us the rooms: they're marvellous, with high ceilings, a bit kitsch for our taste but very affordable. Once installed, we freshen up and change. As dusk falls, we go out for a stroll along the streets, probably the most atmospheric in all of Sicily.

From the farthest reaches of antiquity, although Ortygia was a key location for the Phoenicians and Greeks, its true foundation was due to the Corinthians. It was surrounded by colonies in the interior and was erected as the capital of Magna Grecia. At its height it adopted some notable names, such as Aeschylus and Pindar, and it even managed to defeat Athens in one conflict. Next would come the Carthaginian assault and the Roman siege, giving Archimedes the opportunity to try his celebrated war machines, though nothing could stop Rome sacking the town and taking the riches from its temples. There were many other occupations: Vandals, Goths, Byzantines and Arabs. There were also the Normans, who moved the capital to Palermo, only for it to be returned to Syracuse under the Aragonese. Carlos V reinforced the walls surrounding the island in order to repel Berber pirates. If such misfortunes weren't enough, poverty generated by abusive taxes, the plague and earthquakes all took their toll between the fifteenth and eighteenth centuries. It wasn't until the nineteenth century that the city began to return to something like its original state, a prosperous and happy place. This terrible parade of aggressors, lasting for centuries, hasn't stopped Syracuse smiling on us this evening.

'Syracuse ... even the name sounds lovely!' says Ro, as she starts to hum a song by her beloved Yves Montand: '*Syracuuuuuse ...*'

Leonardo Sciascia, an islander from the interior, must have also liked the town and its name. 'For a Sicilian from the centre, Syracuse keeps an oriental ornament within its syllables,' he once said. 'Right there, the hard, coarse and humble Sicily discovers that the lights have been switched on and sounds orchestrated. The Sicilian distrusts any intimacy with nature. And Syracuse seems to encapsulate a symbol, a secret sacrifice of achieved intimacy.' We are still to learn about central Sicily, and I'm not sure if I understand the last idea, the symbol of intimacy, but I have no doubt that Syracuse is a love at first sight, an instantaneous happiness which kidnaps the senses.

We skirt by the Marina, the berth for enormous yachts, with its bargain book stalls, and continue along the Foro Italico, full of pedestrians at this hour of the evening. A sailing boat cruises across in front. Among the cement-block wave breakers upturned into the sea, little green pools of water are forming. The last rays of light float on the horizon. At the foot of the wall, a few disorientated ducks, fugitives from the beautiful Arethusa fountain, peck at shreds of moss.

'Arethusa, the nymph who won the heart of the hunter Alpheus,' says Ro in a scholarly tone. 'According to Ovid, Virgil and the other poets, the goddess Artemis changed her into a fountain so that her suitor, who by the looks of it was a bit heavy, would stop plaguing her. However, the guy was so tenacious, whilst changed into a subterranean river, he followed her here all the way from Greece until he could mix with her waters.'

'And there was nobody around to impose a restraining order,' harrumphs Ka.

We decide to play one of the most suitable games for getting to know Ortygia and wander at random through its streets. We turn our backs to the sea and loose ourselves in what could be the medieval part of Cádiz, although a little more decayed and dark. If, as Ro says, Palermo is the capital of scaffolding, Messina of *arancini* and Reggio of shop windows, then Syracuse is without doubt the capital of balconies. To walk around with your eyes pegged to the pavements is an unpardonable sin.

One of its primordial delights, if not the best, is to raise your line of sight and take in the thousand balconies dignifying the façades, which seem to crackle like baking bread in front of our eyes, shaping a vertical reliquary. Even the simplest have some detail, design or figure ennobling them. A modern-day poet whom I like a great deal, the Pole Adam Zagajewski, speaks of them in one of his poems dedicated to the island:

> City with the loveliest name, Siracusa;
> don't let me forget the dim
> antiquity of your side streets, the pouting balconies
> that once caged Spanish ladies ...

It's a shame that speculative urbanisation, as much here as Spain, threatens the balcony as an architectural element with extinction. The scandalously overpriced metre-squared floor space doesn't seem prepared to allow itself this luxury, turning such a feature into an unobtainable goal.

After toing and froing we reach Piazza Archimedes, presided over by the Artemis fountain; Diana the huntress sculptured by Giulio Moschetti at the end of the nineteenth century. Although my pulse doesn't race when writing, excusing *Michelangelos* and *Berninis*, it's one of the most attractive sculpted ensembles I have seen and I experience a sense of profound aesthetic pleasure as I observe the tension produced by the delicate centre of the goddess, against the savage foreshortening of the accompanying tritons and sirens.

Twin of Apollo, accomplice to the animals, and moon deity, Artemis has given much material to art and literature. So I once again lash my friends with a Borgesian quote:

> I know that the moon, for Shakespeare, was less the

moon than Diana and less Diana than that obscure little word which lingers: moon.*

'That obscure little word which lingers ...' someone repeats, whilst looking for the astral body in the sky, until finding it, beautifully hanging above the head of the goddess. For once, and without it setting a precedent, nobody counterattacks with an anti-Borgesian reproach.

We retrace our footsteps through the little oval of alleyways until we stop in the Piazza del Duomo, a tremendous arc open to relaxed families, flirting adolescents and passing visitors. Excepting the Piazza del Campo in Siena, I don't know a public space as perfect as this one. The sense of spaciousness, of *air* given by any one of its entrances, is unique to the genre. Even its night-time illumination, which for many would be insufficient, creates a beautiful game of backlit silhouettes among the strollers.

Our cinephile Ka notes that the majority of *Malena* was set here. The film, at times tender and cruel, starred Monica Bellucci who played the haughty leading role. Although her grandiose beauty tends to eclipse all around it, if one focuses on the details it's unmistakable: the Piazza del Duomo was without doubt the location for the great Tornatore's tale of human misery and redemption. The film also reminds us that Sicily was punished heavily by bombing during the Second World War. Where, today, we see the slow figures of pedestrians, the director draped the threatening shadows of aeroplanes. I suddenly, although only for an instant, feel my hair stand on end. The sudden shiver changes into a strange mixture of indignation and sadness, which quickly fades away.

---

* Borges is using classical and Shakespearian imagery involving the moon, and the sound of the word in English. The original Spanish quote is as follows: '*Sé que la luna, para Skakespeare, era menos la luna que Diana y menos Diana que esa obscura palabra que se demora: moon.*'

We approach the cathedral, once a temple in honour of Athena and still with its original columns intact. I've never seen anything similar – and, undoubtedly, if someone had attempted to describe it to me it would have seemed too outlandish an idea – a Greek temple inside a church! Sicily, the land where nothing is what it seems, pure and simple.

'For the first time in my life I didn't feel anti-Christian,' wrote Durrell when he visited the place. Many who visit the Mezquita in Cordoba or the Giralda in Seville think something similar. There's no doubt that the Catholic Church knows how to renovate buildings. In Syracuse the cathedral's façade, a startling yet sumptuous baroque mask, greets whoever comes to sit on its steps.

At the foot of the pavement, living statues, trinket sellers and circus performers gather their public. However, a lamp off to one side remains isolated, with nobody walking by, as if lit in order to pay homage to loneliness. Ro and I exchange a knowingly complicit glance, 'Let's go!', and we run to throw our arms around it together, to bathe under its orphan rays while we emulate Gene Kelly with some rather clumsy choreography.

Iván suggests that it would be a good idea to find something to eat, preferably as economical as possible. Distrusting of the signs proclaiming well-priced menus, we are on the brink of entering a restaurant or *tavola calda* on various occasions, but with as many again, we resist altogether. Some mysterious force drives us away from the terraces and obliges us to keep looking. Finally, we come across a rather faded illumination: Ristorante Nuovo RO.

'New "Ro"?'

'Let's stop right here!' we all say joyously. 'This can't fail us.'

And we weren't wrong. Without it being haute cuisine, which wouldn't have been remotely important anyway, we eat copiously without worrying about the bill: a fresh and fruity moscato wine from the province, spaghetti with broccoli and fillets of sword fish done in the Siracusan style, with garlic, oregano and cinnamon.

'What we call chance is nothing more than our profound ignorance of the rules that govern our destiny' – how true Maestro Borges.

We take a long after-dinner stroll back to the hotel, this time towards the east. I'm exhausted, but delightfully happy, with the irrepressible desire to run about naked shouting 'Eureka! Eureka!' just like the Siracusan Archimedes, beloved of Physics professors and swimming pool manufacturers, who did just that along these very streets.

THE GENEROUS LIGHT pouring through the windows announces the dawn. Very tired, we go down for breakfast. At a nearby table, a group of Syracusans are gathered. They all differ in age and appearance: a bearded man with a tie, a red-headed girl, a young lad with a sharp gaze, an aged man with the air of an old sea dog, a young blondish boy, another man who joins them ... From the manner in which they greet the waiter, they must be from here. I amuse myself by picturing them as a group of superheroes or conspirators on a special mission, or so it seems.

An elderly German woman asks permission to sit next to us and, while she drinks her coffee with audible slurps, starts to read aloud a spiel in her own language. Above the cups and half eaten *cornetti*, I manage to read among her papers the name Schiller. The traveller Joachim Fest, in the *Sicilian Sketches* from his book *Backlit*,* made the assertion that for many Germans 'Syracuse only lives on in a ballad by Schiller'. It's somewhat inexplicable how this lady is stubbornly buried in her text, without realising she is surrounded by the original, real-life model. Though, I suppose, it is rather

---

* The original *Im Gegenlicht* was published in Spain as *A contraluz* (*Backlit*).

similar to what I'm doing, carrying so many notes and quotes. OK, I tell myself, I guess one travels with literature, *one is there.*

Leaving behind Ortygia for Terra Firma, we head towards the Archaeological Park. The route, it could be said, seems decidedly lacking in marvels. The traffic is much heavier than on Ortygia, and the façades infinitely more vulgar. To the right, we make out an unattractive cone, rounded off with a star, finally recognisable as a church, although it appears to be more of a homage to Soviet astronauts. We also pass under a huge banner, hung from one side of the street to the other, asking for help in quashing the Mafia by combating silence and forgetfulness. The inscription contains the names of the most well-known victims of this scourge, trailing off with three disturbing dots: a resigned admission that it will continue.

One of the worst and most problematic aspects of the Mafia is its diffuse nature, like the ugliness spoken of by Italo Calvino. And at times, it's as confused as its etymology, which nobody seems to be able to agree upon. Born as a resistance force against Charles of Anjou's French invaders, it didn't take long to become an extensive system of self-management. It worked with terrifying effectiveness, until some of the forces of law and order decided to take it for what it was, an issue of power and money, and refused to let themselves be bought or blackmailed. They rounded up the most famous *capos* and to a large extent managed to neutralise its power, although evidently so many centuries of perversion can't be resolved at a stroke. I suppose that the practices and attitudes of the Mafia are so deeply rooted in the popular imagination, from its sense of honour to its peculiar rules, that the average Sicilian would have to make a serious effort to free himself from the last vestiges of what is, frankly, a deplorable vernacular culture.

Falcone and Borsellino, the most celebrated martyrs of the anti-Mafia cause, believed it was possible to eradicate the organisation, and it cost them their lives to convince their compatriots that they weren't chasing a chimera. I wonder what all the towns on the island are hoping for by naming squares and avenues after these two. Italo Calvino could well have been thinking about them when he wrote the following: 'The inferno of the living is not something that will be; if there is one, it is what is already here, the inferno where we live every day, that we form by being together. There are two ways to escape suffering from it. The first is easy for many: accept the inferno and become such a part of it that you can no longer see it. The second is risky and demands constant vigilance and apprehension: seek and learn to recognise who and what, in the midst of the inferno, are not inferno, then make them endure, give them space.' A masterly formula that, when applied to Sicily, has allowed the air to become gradually more breathable. Let's hope there continues to be more space for those who aren't part of the inferno.

Meanwhile, for foreign visitors, who have never been the object of attacks or even minor aggression, the simple mention of the Mafia evokes a kind of exciting idiosyncrasy. The invisibility, the law of silence, has played into the hands of violence. Maupassant, who travelled happily through these parts, was surprised by the island's bad reputation: 'Moral: if you're looking for cut-throats, go to Paris or London, but do not come to Sicily,' he affirmed. It's a very wide spread attitude among tourists. Safe from crime, poverty and hunger, these scourges disappear before their very eyes or acquire irresistibly exotic hues.

Literature and the cinema have also been too obliging with the criminals, elevating them to the stuff of legend. And although being portrayed as wretched, they never took the same trouble to clean their image as they did to clean their money. Sciascia, himself, who dedicated some magnificent texts to repelling the ways of the Mafia, never suffered threats from the *Cosa Nostra,* which perhaps shows that in addition to being despicable these characters are also far from being well read.

We reach the Archaeological Park, where we begin our visit at the Greek Theatre. Apart from a few missing tiers it seems to be well preserved. They held the traditional Greek assemblies here, as well as opening performances of dramatic works by Sophocles, Euripides and the adopted Syracusan Aeschylus. Today, they still put on a programme of performances during the high season. The arrival of the Vandals led to its neglect, Charles V then used its stones to reinforce Ortygia's walls. Finally, the erection of mills in the *cavea*, driven by the water redirected from the Anapo River, seriously damaged the configuration of the theatre. The need for restoration only prevailed a couple of centuries ago, and today it glows with an acceptably recovered sparkle.

We walk along next to what little remains of the neighbouring Geron Arch, imagining the bloody sacrifices, up to 400 oxen a day according to historians, and then move on towards the nearby caves. The Ropemakers' Cave is closed, but not so the Ear of Dionysius, a spectacular cavity christened by Caravaggio. Inside, even the slightest noise is amplified like a sound box. As there are few tourists at this early hour, we cheerfully indulge in some shouting, and our voices are lifted up along the wall to the point where the rock is folded like a counterpane under a bed. The tyrant Dionysius – famous for the Sword of Damocles episode and for selling Plato as a slave, a gem of a dictator – locked up his prisoners here and, supposedly, took advantage of the acoustic conditions to eavesdrop their conversations.

Ro also notices that the height of the cave produces a certain feeling of imbalance in the visitor. And, by a rather charming coincidence, our sense of balance is restored by our hearing. However, there are some other interpretations: 'The echo is prodigious. And it suggested immediately the cave of the Cumaean sibyl', writes Durrell. 'But our guide had other notions, based on the fact that the issue of the cave comes out just above the prompter's place in the Greek theatre and he seemed convinced that the two things are somehow connected. The cave for him was a sort of sound box – his image is the case of a violin or the body of the cicada. As far as I could understand his notion the echo of the cave lent strength to the acoustics of the theatre – but somehow this pretty theory seemed to me a little doubtful'. The author of the *Alexandria Quartet* would obviously prefer the sibylline version.

We subsequently visit the catacombs of San Giovanni, excavated underneath an attractive Byzantine church with only a few columns and the three apses still standing. I'm not sure if this has any bearing on our characters but, as much as my friends love crypts, they provoke feelings of anxiety in me very similar to claustrophobia. I'm delighted to find Durrell on my side; although recognising the structure as rather impressive, and it is, he affirms that 'a coal-mine would have offered the same spectacle, really'.

The only thing that distracts me is to imagine the presence here, not of Christians in hiding during the Roman Empire, but of war refugees who sought shelter in these catacombs. And, I don't know why, but I ponder the possibility of a poet being among them who was determined to fill the space with verse. This inspired cave scribbler pervades my imagination as we walk around the galleries between the faded frescos, damp niches and slimy lizards. My friends are concentrating on the guide's explanations; I can't wait to return to the light.

TOGETHER AGAIN in the guests' kitchen of the Hotel Philadelphia, we prepare a copious salad and *farfalle* with fresh tomatoes. The lunch passes quietly, as we discuss trivial matters that drift towards a common worry: the conflicts currently monopolising all the front pages and prompting rivers of ink and saliva in the media. It's reasonable that Islamic fundamentalism is preoccupying Europe, and we're all certainly opposed to any form of violent intransigence, whether derived or not from dogmatic beliefs. However, we're just as scared of the handful of fanatics who call for the persecution of writers as we are of the narrow-minded and malicious people who would have us believe that Islamic culture is, by definition, a source of reaction and terror.

For an Andalusian, and we would imagine also for a Sicilian, the Arab world, supposedly so remote and strange, is part of our very core being. In the south of Spain and Italy, the Arab world revolutionised agriculture, made use of the Roman hydraulic systems to develop irrigation, strengthened commerce and created an environment for the flowering of arts and sciences. Having remembered all this, who would complain? Our cities still share a delightfully familial air with theirs; the colour of our skin, our facial features, and many of our characteristics are due to their legacy. With such a divisive world proposed, thousands of lives are not only going to be sacrificed; we also run the risk of squandering, perhaps forever, a part of ourselves.

It makes me think of Leonardo Sciascia's beautifully written novel, *The Knight and Death*. The story starts with the death of a certain Sandoz, followed by the usual search for suspects. A self-styled group emerges, the Sons of the Eighty-Nine, who never existed before the murder and now lead to all manner of speculations among the police and media. One of the agents investigating the case, at one pertinent moment, asks a worrying question: 'Were the Children of Eighty-Nine created to murder Sandoz, or was Sandoz murdered to create the Children of Eighty-Nine?' And later on he draws a still more startling conclusion: 'Somebody thought they were necessary. There has to be a devil before there can be holy water.'

It's no coincidence these anxieties assail us here in Sicily. For quite a while we've all thought that the old, tired Europe has to abandon some of the ridiculous models that have pushed it towards modernity and look again, even for a while, towards the Mediterranean, the azure cradle of culture. All the hypocritical propaganda about a clash of civilisations loses its perverse meaning here, but still threatens to frustrate the hope of reunion. 'Sicily is the key to everything,' said Goethe, prompting a continuous stream of central European Romantics to visit this land in search of their roots, to try and find themselves. Do today's travellers to Sicily ask themselves where they come from and who they are?

Joachim Fest, who followed Goethe around the island like a good German, also posed a similar question. In the historical backwardness of the south, he managed to see an unexpected advantage: 'The day when Europe's cultural decadence reaches the periphery of the continent, for so long lagging behind, and then destroys everything conserved by such backwardness for centuries, Sicily could also be the key that closes everything'. I would like to think that Sicily is still a key. But a key that opens something.

Our conversation continues as we try to avoid the sad truth: it's nearly time to leave Syracuse. We pack our travel bags, ensuring we don't leave anything in our rooms. But we can't say goodbye without succumbing to a final whim: to dive into the waters that surround Ortygia. Ready with bermudas, bikinis and towels, we go down along the Lungomare di Levante. Its large prism-shaped rocks, anchored in the sea like stony barges, act as barbecues for the Syracusans who like to toast in the sun more than bathe. Iván and I, doing the opposite, launch ourselves into the sea, emulating Jacques Cousteau.

WHILE I DRY OFF in the sun, I read something by Simonides of Ceos, who spent his last days here in Syracuse. Borges quotes him in *Funes the Memorious* as the inventor of mnemonics, the tried and tested method for maximising the potential of your memory. There are those who use it to remember a name or a phone number, but I'd like to put it into practice to recall the number of paving stones we are leaving behind, the exact pigments of the sky waving us off, the precise configuration of the faces that pass by our side. I'd like to be a mnemonic virtuoso in order to retain the name of all the doors, windows, limestone façades shining in the sunset, and so many of the other details too, but it would be all in vain, as this city seems simply unforgettable.

⌁

In this shot, Borges is laughing. There aren't too many photographs of him laughing. And none I remember where he's doing it in such a spontaneous manner: the head thrown back, his body contracted in an implosive guffaw. I can't place it for sure, but I'd bet that the image was taken on the terrace of his Palermo hotel, the Villa Igiea – recognisable from the drooping leaves of the palm and the shadowy outline of the mountain behind – which we'll see later on. A stone cornice protrudes behind Borges. In front of him, almost out of shot, are the rims of two crystal glasses. And if some smart alec wants to see an easy explanation for the hilarity: the maestro was abstemious.

I ask myself why Borges, paradigm of humour as the exaltation of intelligence, smiled so little, at least in public. I'm delighted to know that Michel Foucault wrote *The Order of Things* after a fit of ferocious laughter brought on by reading a passage of the Argentinean's work. Other readers of Borges have experienced very similar situations. Therefore, it's striking that the Italian Umberto Eco, in his meticulous homage to the maestro, *The Name of the Rose*, chose among his characters a blind librarian who hated laughter, a certain Jorge de Burgos.

Sicilians aren't, given what we've seen up to now, too predisposed to laughing. I'm not saying that they seem overly serious, and they're certainly not inexpressive either. Let's just say that they have something of the Mona Lisa about their ambiguous way of displaying happiness. Once again, I look to Fest, who explains it very well: 'The Sicilian smile. I have noticed that on many occasions it only consists of an upturn at the edges of the mouth; less than a smile, more the gesture of a smile. It shows reserve, scepticism and even irony with more intensity than it does any agreement with

Palermo, 1984

the speaker. As if the distance was wholly insurmountable and the stranger was always condemned to remain a stranger.'

Are Sicilians so conditioned by this long series of disasters and curses marking their history? Perhaps, but for many peoples humour is a defence, at times the only one, against misfortune. Ignoring certain slippery practices, it also seems to me that smiling, its older sister – laughter – and its cousins parody, irony, caricature and homage, are ways of being closer to people, and a stranger ought to stop being one as soon as possible. 'The fact of being amused', said Lampedusa in *The Leopard,* 'makes up four fifths of affection'.

However on this island, as we know already, everything has a double face, its reverse side. Italo Calvino used to speak of a comic Sicilian figure, derived from Arabic oral tradition, now spread all over the world: the ingenuous Giufà, the village idiot who always comes up smelling of roses. After taking everything literally, every situation he gets involved in becomes an entertaining trap for those surrounding him. Gaetano Savatteri, the brilliant journalist of Sicilian origin, sees the character as a model of resistance against hypocrisy: 'A burst of laughter buries any lies, whereas Giufà with his smile, either too stupid or too clever, eternally repeats his ingenuous errors.' Comedy as exorcism, as a weapon. The carnival participants from my country also know something of this, makers of jokes on a grand scale.

I also believe that literature and philosophy have explained tears much better than laughter. The muse Melpomene is much more familiar and intelligible to us than Thalia. In any given moment we would know what words or events depress us, but would hesitate when trying to describe what makes us laugh. Neither Aristotle, nor Hobbes, nor Freud, nor even Pirandello have managed to do anything more than approximate the ever so secret contact which ignites the spark of laughter within us. Even Borges wasn't able to get that much further.

'But, it seems much much easier to make someone laugh than to make them cry,' says Iván. 'Any clown in the crowd can tell a funny story. Yet, nobody dares to offer up a tragic performance these days, for fear they'll be laughed at.'

'Don't forget that the best jokes are told during wakes,' interrupts Ro. 'At times the most terrible things, death, chaos, have such an effect on us that we can't find a better way of assimilating them than laughter.'

'Absolutely,' agrees Iván. 'When things don't go as we want, we say that it's a twist of fate, that fate is playing *tricks* on us. The question is whether we're laughing at these things or whether they're laughing at us.'

'Who or what pushed the Argentinean's humour button that day?'

'Unless Scianna or the inseparable Kodama happened to remember it, I fear we'll never know,' says Ka.

I return to the little red book, Scianna does remember. They're telling Borges about D'Annunzio's definition of Marinetti: 'a cretin with flashes of imbecility'. Borges explodes into the already famous fit of laughter. 'Magnificent, magnificent,' he enthuses. 'I used to know another: a *phosphorescent cretin*. Beautiful as well, no? Because in the end, even at night ... But D'Annunzio's is more ingenious. Nevertheless, *phosphorescent* is a magnificent word, don't you think?'

I keep the secret from the others, fearing they won't find it funny. However, realising how precious we've all become talking about this, some of us naturally start to laugh, which ends up spreading until we all crack up, as if drunk with happiness.

Catania

IT ENDED UP being a cheerfully sociable night, enlivened with a rich vein of Lambrusco and rum chasers. At home, Ro read some of her satirical poems, Iván danced with Ka, and I unfolded my repertoire of imitations including lesser and more well-known poets, plus a few novelties that were unfailingly mediocre parodies of Borgesian style.

Outside, the Calabrian coast was once again glittering, beautiful in contrast to the strident neons of the churches, which in Messina vie with the pubs and nightclubs for the bad taste crown. The day had been a long one, and we had arrived in Via Noviziato Casazza with a real feeling of returning home, to home sweet home – protective, familiar and ours.

However, earlier on we had been to Catania, its big city profile unfurling along the roadsides and through the lemon groves, as the radio-cassette of our Fiat Panda (now baptised 'Eureka') reeled off the songs of Mina. Her sounds of the seventies and *la-la-las* are just about tolerable for mitigating the mind-numbing havoc of a traffic jam:

> *Ho fatto un buco nella sabbia*
> *per nascondere tutto quello*
> *che ho nel cuore per te ...**

---

* The lyrics literally translate as 'I've made a hole in the sand to hide everything I have in my heart for you ...'

I have to say that Catania, a city I had barely been able to make out from the air, awakens in me an irrational, almost allergic rejection. In my imagination, the difference between Syracuse and Catania was the same that exists between light and darkness. However much I learned of its active cultural life or architectural riches, and although the people here appear friendlier than in other places, without doubt I found it the least appealing city on the island. Our brief visit didn't noticeably alter this prejudice; on the contrary, it only confirmed my gut reaction.

That being said, it's no impediment to recognising Catania's admirable resistance to all kinds of catastrophe. From the devastating earthquake of 1693, to the dozens of Etna's eruptions (its terrifying near neighbour), which have buried entire districts, nature has felt no need to show any mercy with its excessive furies. Time and again Catania has had to straighten itself up with heroic obstinacy. Not even the persuasions of the Jesuits, who saw the crater as the entrance to the flames of hell, managed to expel the Catanese from their land. The last volcanic activity took place during the previous November, and Ro used to tell me of the mountains of ash that she'd sweep from her balcony in Messina every day. In Catania, this grey film now covers the buildings with a patina of sadness and squalor.

We stop Eureka's engine near to the Porto Vecchio and come to a little fruit market. A quick look around is enough to confirm what Etna the destroyer has made possible, via an age-old process of sedimentation, creating the unusual fertility of the surrounding land. Ka reckons this is why the director Jean-Claude Lauzon in his poetic film *Leolo* made his protagonist the son of a Sicilian tomato, who had accidentally impregnated a woman!

On the subject of tomatoes, the customer can choose from four or five varieties, each one more wholesome than the last. The assistant throws me a wary look when I ask her in my impoverished Italian the difference between them.

'These here are one type and those over there are another.'

As I don't need provisions on this journey, only tomatoes to nibble on, I choose those seemingly most suitable for salads. We also get a shiny *melone*, specifically a watermelon, and some peaches and grapes. We load Eureka's boot and enter the city on foot through the Porto Uceda, as dark as a cave at this time of day.

OUR MAIN OBJECTIVE is the false robbery report that we didn't manage in Messina. Although we're too tense to admire the palaces we're stumbling upon, I discover that the darkness of the façades isn't due to the intermittent dustings of ash. Or not only due to that. In fact almost the entirety of the old town of Catania was built with black stone from the volcano at the end of the seventeenth century. It's admirable to think how the terrible neighbour has been something more than just a force for destruction; it has even offered up materials to enable the city to once again stand on its own two feet.

Guided by an endless series of contradictory signs, we get to the police headquarters. A receptionist invites us to take a seat in the waiting room, where among other notices we read:

False reports will be punished by penalties
of up to three years in prison.

Now we don't need to feign compunction, we swallow hard.

Luckily, the police looking after us aren't too stern. One of them seems annoyed that we've interrupted his game of solitaire on the computer. The other, who was watching television, is very talkative. He claims to know something of Spain, he slyly flirts with the girls and even allows himself to make some recommendations for our visit to the south of the island. During a period of interminable minutes, we mechanically agree to everything, until Ka is handed a copy of the form.

'Heh I've got my pirate's license!' she shouts, once we're a safe distance from the lion's mouth.

In order to celebrate we head towards the cathedral. We pass a lit patio that attracts us by its decrepitude. It's enigmatically called *La Collegiata*, like the sumptuous Basilica Collegiata, the royal Aragonese chapel also built in the town, although a poorer version. A rare irony, I tell myself. Further on, in the centre of the main square, an elephant sculpted from the ubiquitous volcanic stone supports an obelisk with Egyptian inscriptions; apparently the Catanese are very proud of it and see it as a symbol of intelligence and longevity. I'm beginning to understand nothing: building sites with the name of a basilica, Egyptian elephants ... The city bewilders me, makes me impatient, and I start to make noises about it getting late.

Without paying me the slightest attention, the others look for a *pasticceria*. They want to try some of the sweet confections resembling fruit we've seen in numerous windows. We hope that the flavour justifies the price, which isn't exactly cheap. However, when we plough through our faux apple, cherry and prickly pear, we realise they all taste exactly the same; like marzipan decorated with caramel syrup, rather sickly sweet. The locals call them *frutta martorana*.

'Well,' I say, gently mocking my companions, 'if a baroque façade can hide a Greek temple, why can't a fruit contain marzipan? We're in Sicily my friends, Pirandellism elevated to its highest level.'

WE STROLL THROUGH the Catanese night between open-air jazz concerts, bar terraces and book stalls. A group of youngsters shamelessly check out Ka and Ro, wolf-whistling and offering up some unintelligible flirtatious comments. They ignore them and walk on by.

I've thought a lot about the famous Don Juan tendencies attributed to Italian men, the compulsive and often infantile inclination towards the amorous conquest, which is not without an inkling of truth. Most commonly applied to those from the south, it's not for nothing that Molière wanted his Don Juan to be Sicilian; he was well aware of the legend from Italian sources long before hearing of the *Burlador* from Tirso de Molina.

A great writer little known in Spain, the Syracusan Vitaliano Brancati masterfully highlights the phenomenon in his work *Don Giovanni in Sicily*, an enjoyable tale also with its fair share of tragedy. It reflects the impossibility of coming close to the mystery of woman, but taken to the extreme of pathological obsession, young men condemned to spend their lives between frustration and braggadocio. Lampedusa, for his part, used to joke about an acquaintance of his who was somewhat indiscrete when boasting of his conquests, wondering 'whether he'd screw with a stopwatch in his hand'. He also used to talk about the obsessive topic of the cuckold, or unfaithful spouse – always someone else's drama, a joke at another's expense – as 'the hub around which the island's life turns'. In the delightful and realistic films of Tornatore, such as the aforementioned *Malena* or the moving *Cinema Paradiso*, allusion to infidelity is never far away or, for that matter, the desperate persecution of young women and onanistic adolescents caught in the cinema.

I think that there's a fair bit of disguised repression in these outbursts, a dash of histrionics, and a touch of mechanical apathy. And as some Pirandello experts have pointed out, there could be a yearning for multiplicity; the desire to be *one hundred thousand*. It's often said about adultery that it needs a 'double life'; project this onwards to the limits of promiscuity and one finds oneself again when feeling like *no one*. Or there are times when you want *everyone* to be *no one* before you commit to *one*. Complex emotional arithmetic, but nobody said that love was an exact science.

WOLF WHISTLES and salacious comments irritate Ka. She sees them as intolerable macho aggressiveness. Are the Sicilians male chauvinists; are they worse in this respect than, for example, the average Spaniard? The matriarchal structure has prestige here, but everybody knows that some women, too, can be faithful guardians of the most execrable machismo. And returning to Brancati, he went as far as saying about one of his characters that 'he was Spanish, which is as good as saying Sicilian'. Could he also have been talking about this very typical satyriasis? Lacking further information, we'd better leave the debate at this juncture.

Savatteri, always astute, makes the point that the island's rich literature doesn't have, by any means, an Anna Karenina or a Madame Bovary; the female characters are only shadows of the men, ghosts wandering around the home without playing a larger role. The exception proving the rule could have been Maria Messina, the Sicilian Katherine Mansfield, a heroine from the end of the nineteenth century who in her stories and novels denounced the atmosphere of seclusion felt by the island's women. A swift illness took her too soon, she was forgotten, and was rescued for posterity as a disciple of Giovanni Verga. I think this too flattering a verdict for the author of *The House of the Medlar Tree*. Messina surpassed him in rhythm, depth and precision of language. But she was a woman, and that was the price she paid.

On the other hand, the Italian idea of sexuality is a mystery to us. You have the refined eroticism of Boccaccio, the extreme visions of Fellini and Pasolini, the repressive mechanisms of Opus Dei and the Vatican, and the porn star Rocco Sifredi! Unexpectedly, Italy, it seems, has a whole heap of flesh, celluloid, ink on paper and ecclesiastical purple where the female libido appears to have little to say, being reduced to the same target for casanovas and inquisitors.

This may be why there was such a scandal when a sixteen-year-old Catanese, Melissa Panarello, revolutionised the editorial market by publishing *One Hundred Strokes of the*

Brush Before Bed, an intimate diary where, given her age, she itemised her more than daring sexual experiences. Another local, the actress and writer Goliarda Sapienza, writes with no less success in *The Art of Joy* about bedroom antics with both men and women, and the libertine behaviour of a girl born in a poor and disapproving Sicily.

As a literary work, I much prefer Sapienza's book. In a way, the story deals with liberty, the role of sexuality in personal development and individual dignity. *One Hundred Strokes* seems suspiciously precocious, of little interest, and in reality light years from *Lolita* or *Bonjour tristesse*, with which it has been compared. However, a Sicilian adolescent girl talking about sex has proved a very profitable commotion for her publishers! And so it continues, selling thousands of copies, quickly leading to an announcement of a forthcoming film version.

In the book there's a ballad in dialect:

> At night Catania so lovely seems,
> Shining beneath the bright moonbeams.
> The mountaintop is red with fire;
> Its heat to lovers proves most dire.

Tiny volcanoes starting to erupt as night falls, surrounding the Mother Volcano watching it all. But the flames of lust, as Sciascia noted, don't always relate to sensuality. I'm not condemning one in favour of the other, God forbid! I'm only saying that at times the same distance exists between the two as exists between imagination and the facts, between reality and desire.

Unable to get aroused by Catania (for we also get sensual and sentimental stimuli from cities, even certain possessive impulses, including lascivious ones), I still want to get out of here as soon as possible. I don't know why; the others tell me it's not so bad, just to enjoy the stroll. But, even now, as I write these lines, I don't feel any pleasure from my recollections of travelling through Catania. Let's hope Saint Agatha, the infallible patron of the city, forgives me.

Finally, I manage to convince my friends; we return to Eureka and I agree to be Ka's co-driver. I sigh with absurd relief when we join the *autostrada* on the way to Messina.

Messina, Taormina, Messina

WE AWAKE AT HOME in our Messina base. While Ro goes off to the university to run a few errands, the rest of us decide to visit the cathedral bell tower in order to witness the twelve o'clock bells. We arrive with time to spare and get a good spot in the shade. Little by little the tourists start to cram around the tower, zoom lenses at the ready, the first 'dong' sounds and the cogs start to turn. My friends love the bronze zoo which unfolds above them: roaring lions, clucking chickens, angels suspended in the air, original and picturesque.

Other indigenous fauna attracts my attention instead, a meeting in a nearby corner bar of, according to Ro, young *Mafiosi*. Conditioned by Mario Puzo's novels, I once thought of them as formally dressed enigmatic men with ceremoniously slow manners that hid, under this noble appearance, bloody crimes of mythic proportions. From what I can make out, without being too obvious, the customers gathered in this café are no less vulgar than any other gang of delinquents the world over. Expensive and tasteless shirts, thick gold chains around their neck and wrists, sun glasses, contemptuous and boastful gestures. Once again I think how those who combated the damaging legend of an honourable society were right. Borges had fancied he could see such a society, a heroic caste, amongst the cut-throats from Buenos Aires. Perhaps a trigger-happy nature, ambition and barbarity never give rise to epic figures outside of literature, only to rogues of the worst kind.

In reality, all those who visit Sicily are well aware of its fascination with death – an enduring feature that has been around for goodness knows how long. Earthquakes, eruptions, battles, sacking of cities are all frequent landmarks in its history. The worst tyrants took control and subdued the population by very bloody methods. One of the island's oldest traditions is the *pupi*, the Carolingian puppet theatre regularly held in many towns with great success, and which could not be further removed from the cuddly puppets of Sesame Street. They stage battles to the sound of the barrel organ, where it's not uncommon to see the characters cut in two by a sword, heads and limbs flying in all directions whilst the public applaud.

The churches are full of chilling relics. Even Fest and Fulco di Verdura pointed out the fact that presents are not brought by the Three Wise Men or Santa Claus, but by the deceased, specifically on the Day of the Dead. We've seen many streets on the island plastered with obituary notices, announcing a bereavement, noting an anniversary, thanking people for their condolences or for medical care received. It is even said that the custom of preparing your own gravestone still survives, given the argument that it's better to coexist with death than deny it. Or, according to one of Sciascia's characters, to make sure that one rests 'in a dry place' for all eternity.

Each time I come down the stairs of the apartment, rather than waiting for the coffin substitute otherwise known as the building's lift, I stop to reread the notice a neighbour has pinned on the door in remembrance of his dearly departed wife.

'It's been here at least nine months, since I came. A long period of mourning,' Ro assures me with apprehension.

How can a place such as this, so full of light and life, end up paying homage to the cult of death, a death that, whether by the hand of man or from nature's excesses, is almost always violent, cruel or harsh? I remain without an answer. Unless I accept the incredible explanation put forward by Pirandello: 'Almost all Sicilians have an instinctive fear of life ... They are distrustfully aware of the contrast between their closed soul and the nature surrounding them, open, full of sun, and they withdraw still further into themselves ...'

I've only once heard someone say to me that he didn't fear death, but life. It was in an interview with a Spanish poet more famous for having spent his life in a psychiatric hospital than for his tremendous verses. Is Pirandello right? Could this blessed isle be a mental hospital disguised as paradise? I resist the thought, however much an overt reverence for death jumps out at me from every corner.

Ro arrives back in a bad mood, let down by the administration. In the local university, as often happens in Spanish ones, everything is slow and bogged down with bureaucratic obstacles. In order to help her relax, and foreseeing the heat that awaits us, we have a *granita* and get ready to leave for near-by Taormina, the town of the bull.

Its history isn't so different from the others we've visited. A Greek enclave, followed by a Roman colony, it eventually became the capital of Byzantine Sicily. The Arabs initially destroyed it only then to pamper it, promoting the development of agriculture in its surroundings. The Normans benefited from this prosperity and the aristocracy put up numerous palatial residences. The good fortune seemed to last, but during the Second World War the bombardments weren't to be sneezed at: the clear sky in front of us now was once full of merciless fire. The impetus of tourism, an easily forecastable gold mine, has enabled this brutal past to fade from memory. Today the invaders don't carry cutlasses and rifles, but smart phones and endless supplies of euros. We have neither one nor the other, but are still inclined not to miss out on a visit.

To get to Taormina we have to leave the car in a parking area situated at the base of the mountain, and then take a free shuttle bus to the town. Without such measures, the gridlock would be impossible. In the station I discover (at last!) the first presence of Borges. Although my Italian is deplorable, I place it straight away: it's a quote from *The Garden of Forking Paths* captured on a tourist poster:

FUNVIA TAORMINA MAZZARÒ

*... un uomo puó essere nemico di altri uomini, di
altri momenti di altri uomini, ma non d'un paese:
non di lucide, di parole, di giardini, di corsi d'acqua,
di tramonti.* *

Jorge Luis Borges

We'll soon discover that it's also very difficult to be an enemy of Taormina, of its fireflies, words, gardens, streams of water, sunsets. It's very difficult to be an enemy *in* Taormina. I do a stock take of a few details: the layout of its coquettish streets, still infested with tourists and knick-knack sellers; its vertiginous viewing point sticking out over the Ionian coast, almost giving us the sensation of being suspended in the air; San Giuseppe behind, with the bas-relief of a skull that invites dreams of a fabulous church for pirates; the splintered door of what was the Hotel Metropol; and the impossibly cramped confines of the alleyway Stretto, that's to say Narrow, so much so that Iván photographs it with the greedy intention of sending it to the *Guinness Book of Records*. It all makes the senses skip to a unique beat.

You don't need to stretch the imagination too much to understand that, for decades, this was a meeting place for poets and painters. Goethe, Oscar Wilde and Thomas Mann all visited, and Thomas Bernhard wrote his *Ave Virgilio* in Taormina. Camus may also have known it, as one

---

* '... a man can be an enemy of other men, of the moments of other men, but not of a country: not of fireflies, words, gardens, streams of water, sunsets.'

of the characters in his book *The Fall* talks with familiarity about this part of the island. Moreover, Truman Capote was witness here to an unpleasant encounter, probably the last, between Gide and Cocteau. Among the musicians captivated by Taormina are those of no lesser stature than Brahms (Borges' favourite) and Wagner. Among the painters are the landscape artists headed by Nicolás Poussin.

As you'd expect, it wasn't all gifted virtue during the population's golden years. In a census of the glorious Arts and Letters that made Taormina famous, one figure appears rather sinister for my tastes, a figure who could well have had his own chapter in the *Universal History of Iniquity* along with Billy The Kid and Lazarus Morell. I'm referring to Wilhem von Gloeden, Prussian, self-proclaimed Baron and skilful photographer. His work, homoerotically inspired, quickly circulated throughout the more liberal, or hypocritical, sections of Victorian Europe, which didn't take long in making Taormina its favourite destination. These images were subject to persecution and seizure by Mussolini and the Church; although many negatives were destroyed, the remaining collection is more than considerable.

Naked ephebes are portrayed in natural outdoor settings, isolated or in groups, almost always posing whilst dressed in imitation of Greek antiquity. These are the models of von Gloeden, who awoke not only the interest of lovers of the artistic nude, but also of fellow homosexuals perhaps as interested in the size of the members on show as the focal correction or the treatment of light. The self-same Roland Bathes, although recognising certain technical deficiencies, wrote an essay captivated by this character.

What is stopping me enjoying these photographs? Firstly, I suspect the Baron was never interested in Taormina or its people. He simply found a lost Mediterranean village, with a climate favourable to his pulmonary conditions, a tolerant spirit and country youths willing to pose for him, for who knows what low price. Secondly, there is the fact that the casual models were minors, as is evident in some cases, which raises the question as to whether nineteenth-century art tolerated what one could call conscience-based ethical precepts that would now be classified as child pornography. And last but not least, there are the faces of the boys captured in these works, with their expression deadened or anaesthetised so they resemble puppets before Gloeden's perverse lens, however much toga and laurel wreath they're hidden behind.

With or without legitimacy von Gloeden's output is certainly sold in all of Taormina's souvenir shops, be it as catalogues, posters or postcards. I did acquire one of the latter, one of his few female shots. A portrait of a girl, dressed, leaning against a log. She has strength and beauty, but above all she expresses innocence (those big black eyes) and a certain anxiety (her hand rests on her chest). Von Gloeden didn't like this nameless girl. Her gaze is like an eternal and silent slap in the face.

We visit the magnificent Greek theatre, where Goethe pointed out how 'art has assisted nature'. Today, it still serves as a place for concerts and performances of classical texts, although with no production scheduled at the moment, it offers us another continuously showing spectacle: the sight, from its heights, of the entire region and a vast expanse of sea.

'Seeing a performance here has got to be spectacular,' says Ro, whilst consulting this season's programme. 'Ah, and in a couple of weeks Caetano Veloso's coming!'

Zagajewski, my favourite Pole with apologies to Milosz and Lem, was also here, and he left some lovely epigrammatic verses as witness:

From the theatre in Taormina you spot
the snow on Etna's peak
and the gleaming sea.
Which is the better actor?

From one of the heights I'm reminded of a luminous and colouristic picture by the Parisian Viollet-le-Duc, painted around 1836, who tried to reconstruct the theatre in all its details, as if newly opened, not forgetting the spectators and the actors on stage. It seems he started by outlining what he could see of the deteriorated structure, slowly reinstating lost elements, until his imagination finally exploded and he ended up reinventing what was or could have been here. And the Parisian wasn't the only one to succumb to similar temptations. It's curious and touching this desire to restore, with the aid of fantasy and observation, what time has taken away. However, some modern restorers insist on taking such a desire to intolerable extremes, whether by making ruins more attractive or simply not accepting them as they lie.

It's time to leave town, take control of Eureka and go for a refreshing dip in the sea, which I had wanted to do ever since I spotted the nearby little island, lifted straight from *Peter Pan,* and which the locals call Isola Bella. To get there we go down towards Giardini-Naxos, where the railway station is located, very close to the archaeology bearing ample testimony to the rich Greek colonial past, finally destroyed by Dionysius, the satrap of Syracuse. Today, as with Taormina, it's a tourist attraction of undeniable success, if not over-developed, as you'd find today with any mediocre Spanish beach. The car park is certainly a minefield and we take more than half an hour to find a space. Ka is subjected to a true resit of her driving test in trying to slot the vehicle into a bay without damaging it.

It will be worth the bother. Linked to the beach by a thin strip of sand, marked with private property signs, Isola Bella is covered by a very different species of vegetation, which in good measure contributes to its magical appearance. The surrounding waters are deeper than they seem, and the seabed of rounded stones opens up like a transparent aquarium.

'This is like the Red Sea!' exclaims Iván when coming face to face with the surface.

The temperature is ideal, the surroundings like paradise. As a child I remember having an astronomy book that speculated on a theory concerning the end of the world. It would be an apocalypse following one perfect final day, notable for its ideal temperature. The text was accompanied by an airbrushed illustration of coastal scenery at nightfall that was so calming you almost wished the prophecy would come true as soon as possible. I never believed I would find myself inside such a scene, as I do now, with the added advantage of the world not ending. At least not for the moment.

We have a snack, waiting for the sunset, along with some *ragazzi*, skipping stones over the still water, the bigger the better, whilst a painter dries his panels among the rocks. Time stands still like a peaceful millpond. We're only awoken from the spell when it starts to cool.

We head back to Messina. But before arriving home, we take the car up around the panoramic road above the city, until reaching the viewing point where more than a few couples park their cars and cover the windscreens with cardboard or cloth, in order to steam up the windows away from the gaze of prying eyes. We also happen upon a small but impressive cemetery full of lit candles, like an altar fitted into the side of the mountain. The track takes us to the structure known as the *Pilone*, erected on the beach next to numerous refreshment stalls covered in flies. It's so similar to the Astilleros Dockyard tower standing at the entrance to Cádiz, our very own Eiffel tower.

The view of the strait also reminds me of the Mediterranean city of Ceuta,* bathed by another strait, that of Gibraltar, where all my family originate. This sliver of sea was always a short distance, a pleasant trip spent dolphin spotting or counting the waves breaking over the ferry's hull. Taking this into consideration, it used to amaze me how my friends from

---

* Ceuta is a small Spanish enclave located on the North African side of the Strait of Gibraltar.

Ceuta would always speak of the Peninsula as a rather remote destination, bordering on the unreachable. As they inevitably looked to the strait, a stretch of water always prone to swells closing the port, I suppose the sea must have taken on colossal proportions for them. With time, these scant fourteen kilometres had been virtually multiplied until they became a frontier difficult to cross, above all for the imagination.

A COUPLE OF HOURS LATER we return to base and eat a frugal dinner. Just before going to bed, Iván prepares his notebook next to the nightstand, as he has the habit of writing down his dreams religiously every morning. The girls are also capable of remembering theirs, and for a while we exchange them. But most of the time I can't remember what I've dreamt, and if by chance I do, I always cheat myself as they're never especially narrative dreams, nor laden with symbols like the doors, keys and islands of my friends. So when it comes to my turn, I once again reach for Borges and relate the tale the maestro told of Boethius, who dreamed of being a horse race spectator:

'The animals gather on the start line, they start to gallop, they pass each other, one finally crosses the line first. Then in a flash Boethius sees that there is another dreamer, who is dreaming of him and the horses and the race ...'

A salvo of yawns stops me explaining that this is God, who sees everything but allows providence and free will, etc.

With the lights already switched off, Ro tells me about the other races she has heard of in Messina. Not the official ones of those at the racetrack, but secret meetings, clandestine races. Carriages charging along the city's deserted streets in the small hours, with *Mafiosi* betting fearsome sums. During the night I'll hear them from my room. The wheels and horseshoes drumming on the paving stones, powerfully and rhythmically, until fading away down the hill, towards the deepest sleep.

Messina, Tindari, Castelbuono

WE SET OFF ONCE MORE, this time towards the west of the island; the bass beats of a flamenco guitar, congruous with the landscape, thrums on the stereo. Soon, to one side of the road a miraculous new vista opens up. It would never be more appropriate to describe it as one of those views so beloved of the illustrators of school catechisms: a miracle of golden sands facing the sea, from this height shining like an immense mirror, azure and overpowering.

A sign announces the proximity of Tindari, a former Greek colony, once destroyed by the Arabs and finally a Catholic shrine. We enter the site via a very steep slope, until we reach the enormous natural balcony referred to by Quasimodo,

> I know you gentle in broad hills hung over waters
> of the god's sweet isles;
> today you assail me ...

Vertigo mingles, struggles with mystic pleasure. The sun starts to warm the sea and makes the empty beach gleam; the day is sufficiently clear enough to see Lipari, right there, almost within reach.

THE CATHOLIC CHURCH'S COLONISATION of this corner of the island certainly isn't down to a whim. A legend tells how a boy fell from these heights, and that the Virgin Mary unfurled a providential sliver of sand to gather him up.

'I'd hate to imagine the thud the poor kid produced. A trampoline would've been a better bet,' says Ka looking down.

Thankful for such divine intervention, the parishioners raised a basilica – somewhat unfortunate from an aesthetic point of view as it could be called an architectural monstrosity. But this doesn't stop legions of pilgrims periodically making the trip here. Even the Pope has passed through Tindari, leaving behind a dreadful metallic structure in homage, painted white, a copy of a scrapped space capsule lying abandoned on the grass at the entrance to the grounds.

'It's a shame John Paul II didn't want to repeat the miracle and throw himself, along with that thing, off the embankment. Just to give us an example,' says an anticlerical Iván, always on the side of Liberation Theology. Of all Liberations.

'I don't want to be more antipapist than the Antipope,' I explain in advance, 'but listen: while they didn't forgive Borges for picking up a prize from Pinochet, no do-gooder reproached Wojtyla for giving Holy Communion to the Chilean dictator. I don't like such double standards: we're all Moors, or all Christians!'

'That's impossible in Sicily, where everyone is a Moor and a Christian at the same time,' judges Ro.

Andrea Camilleri, the writer of the Montalbano detective novels, called one of his works *The Excursion to Tindari*. The storyline revolves around the disappearance of an old married couple en route from Agrigento to the shrine. The plot springs to life before our eyes, as the public gradually surrounding us is, in the majority, of pensionable age. Among them I detect a certain Christian fervour, but also a rather indolent, absent-minded inertia.

There is no doubt that Sicily is a very religious island. And especially devoted to Mary: there are so many virgins, more than in Andalucía, and they all have multitudes of devotees.

Pio XII declared the island, in one of his radio broadcasts, 'the domain of the most Holy Mary', and so it has continued right up to the present. I once heard a well-known theology professor give a ridiculous explanation regarding the Marian devotion found in southern Europe. In essence, it referred to the Reconquest's attempt to re-establish the dignity of women, which would have been relegated under the empire of al-Andalus – as if Christianity, from the fifteenth century to the present, has been specifically characterised by its militant feminism.

Of Christs in Sicily, I believe there are less. This may be due to the crucifixion representing salvation through tormented flesh and death, something the Sicilians have already had to endure enough. The miraculous virgins, and even the sorrowful ones, move other kinds of emotion. They intercede in aid of parishioners or share their misfortunes, but they don't spill their blood or expose themselves to sacrificial redemption. But let's be clear, this is all just conjecture. During a visit to a Sicilian church, they say D. H. Lawrence was startled by the realistic details of a martyred Christ. When he asked an old lady the reason for such minute replication, she explained to him that it was because Jesus had made his mother suffer. From the redeemer of humanity to a difficult child crucified, by popular decree.

Although in Spain I flee terrified from incense or bands with bugles and drums, I admit that I'd like to see one of the island's numerous processions. I really have just one thing clear in my mind: from the foundational Greek polytheism to Marian devotion, Sicilian spirituality's display of rites, symbols and invocatory monuments requires as much devotion as it does fear of any wrath descending from the heavens. 'Gods and Monsters' could have been a good motto for the island's coat of arms.

WE LEAVE TINDARI for Cefalù. Once again I'm Ka's co-driver and I tap my fingers on the glove compartment in time to the music. The road is monotonous, the sea on the right-hand side a transparent blue. Gazing aimlessly, we pass nameless villages whose walls are plastered with yellowing circus posters showing the familiar trapeze artists, clowns and wild animals we've noticed before. Ro had wanted to take one we'd seen in Messina, showing the head of a tiger with its jaws open, but Sicilian bill posters are stuck so conscientiously, as if lathered with Loctite, there is no way to remove them in one piece.

'The savage sun / so like the decisive claw of the tiger ...' I recite Borges in a trite, but not exaggerated association of ideas. The potent sun falling on our heads does attack with ferocious claws. It's not the progressive heat of a stove, as is normal in coastal areas from dawn to the height of day, but true bursts from a flame-thrower; the flames of hell fire, which melt the asphalt and blur the lines on the horizon.

Wandering along this side of the coast we notice that engineering works have taken hold of a good part of the island, whether that's an infinity of iron bridges stretching out into the distance, the multiplication of road outlines or long tunnels perforating the mountainsides. Now I understand the tacit joke concerning the family who play a lead role in Vittorini's singular novel *Tune for an Elephant*. One of the characters started to recognise in his grandfather the merit of having carried out all of Sicily's engineering works, and ends up attributing to him the Coliseum in Rome, the Great Wall of China and the Pyramids in Egypt.

Whoever is capable of so much, the author ironically seems to tell us, is capable of so little.

The flaming claws don't cease; the heat is going to beat us into a state of dehydration and our reserves of water are diminishing dangerously, becoming a tepid and undrinkable sludge. Even for those of us used to the dry Levant, this African sirocco is raising temperatures to almost annoying levels.

Ka is showing symptoms of tiredness, Ro says she's feeling carsick. So we pull over by the Castelbuono railway station, completely deserted at this time of day. The ticket office seems empty and closed, and there's no sign of the characteristic signalman's uniform in what is truly a ghost station. After a few minutes of calm, the gusts of burning air return. We decide to look for a bench in the shade.

Ro slowly begins to get her colour back, Ka stretches her legs. Meanwhile Iván entertains himself by bending over the rails trying to hear an approaching train, like the Indians do in films. He stays on all fours for a while, seemingly concentrating hard. When he gets up, I ask him if he's heard anything.

'No, nothing,' he says lifting a hand to his reddened ear, 'but it really burns.'

Cefalù

WE REACH CEFALÙ, with its great head of rock over-looking the sea, as the very name suggests. Or as Durrell said in a rather more long-winded fashion, 'a great whale basking in the blueness – a mythological ruminant of a fish, dreaming of some lost oceanic Eden, its eyes shut'. On entering the town, you soon understand that all the grandiloquence is, as almost always, over the top. It's a framework of whitened tranquil streets, nothing to do with a sleeping Moby Dick or some such fantasy. Ah, writers, so pretentious, so exaggerated, always insisting on poeticising what is already poetical! I guess Iván is right.

Finding a parking space with shade from the sun proves difficult, but essential if we don't want Eureka to melt like a mozzarella under the weighty columns of the sun's rays. After various failed attempts, we park under a rather puny tree, mean with its shadows, and stroll at random through the network of streets. With good reason, hardly anyone is outdoors. The entire town seems to be sleeping through a prolonged siesta, as if the drowsiness had been imposed by municipal decree. From a window I hear an English song that I can't quite recognise. Everywhere smells of summer, warm winds and leisurely hours.

We want to go to the beach featured in all the guides and postcards, but we don't know the way. For those of us who live surrounded by the sea, there is help at hand, something like a sixth sense: wherever we are, we always work out how to get there. With the intuition of a Mediterranean seer, I put my best foot forward, as if I had grown up in these very streets. After rounding a couple of corners the fragrance of saltpetre rises up towards me, along with the unmistakable voices of children playing and a subtle but unmistakable luminous shimmer on the walls.

WE COME TO THE BEACH, with its characteristic stripped down little houses, almost dipping the feet of their balconies along the water's edge. Iván and I go up to the breakwater wall and look for the best angle for our cameras. A light breeze makes us feel a bit better. We spread our towels over the sand and take it in turns to swim and keep watch over the valuables. It all looks very familiar: fathers take a nap under their parasols, mothers scold their small children for venturing too far into the water, a few teenagers smoke clandestine cigarettes among the rocks, under the diminishing shade of the little houses.

Any scribbler of travel books likes to collect out of the ordinary events, frantic incidents, exotic sketches. However, such a charitable and commonplace peace demands, at least, a paragraph filled with pleasure and gratitude.

'One ought to know how to be bored, Orlando,' I say to Iván, quoting Lampedusa. My friend makes a gesture of total agreement.

I look again at the breakwater and don't need Ka to tell me that on this very spot a scene from *Cinema Paradiso* was filmed, which for many is the Sicilian director Guiseppe Tornatore's best film. At this point in the movie, little Totò has already grown up, and as it's summer the screenings take place out in the open. A few boatmen have even launched their boats to avoid buying tickets. The protagonist lies back next to the projector, dreaming of the rather silly girl he hasn't heard from in ages, yet who has won his heart. Meanwhile, on the big screen – situated right where Iván and I are taking photos – Odysseus, or should that be Kirk Douglas, is killing the Cyclops. A storm is suddenly unleashed, all the spectators flee and like providential rain the love of his life falls right into his lap.

'Luckily, it's cloudless today,' says Iván sarcastically. 'Come on, get up, let's go for a walk.'

WE WALK AROUND the tight and twisted streets of Cefalù. One is certainly even narrower than the lane in Taormina, which Iván wanted to send to the *Guinness Book of Records*. We can hardly fit if we tilt to one side and that's with our stomachs clenched. One could call it an architectural barrier for the obese. The surprising thing is how such economy of space dates from a time when inflation didn't so drastically affect the square metre as it does today. Better not give the real estate sharks any ideas.

As is seemingly normal to us now, we discover that Cefalù has had more flags than a conference at the UN. It appears to have Phoenician origins, it was obviously Greek, and also allied to Carthage. In the First Punic War it was betrayed and crushed by the Roman fleet. Absorbed by the empire, it was later occupied by the Arabs until the arrival of the Normans. Cefalù's history is, as with the other towns on our trip, an interminable game of lead soldiers, and each has left more or less eloquent traces.

It's now time to reveal that my friend Iván is a consummate hunter of falsifications. A long time before reading *The Council of Egypt* by Leonardo Sciascia, a real gem of a book about historical distortions, he was already dedicating himself to unmasking frauds only accepted as true by everyone because they were taught in school. When we visit Cefalù Cathedral, begun in 1131, he seems fascinated.

In another complex novel, *The Smile of the Unknown Mariner*, Vincenzo Consolo takes up the legend of the Norman king Ruggero, who left Naples with his fleet and was caught in a fierce storm near Salerno. It's said that he raised his voice in prayer and swore he would build a church for his Saviour where he first touched land, and it was precisely here on the shores of Cefalù that he was able to weigh anchor safe and sound. No sooner said than done, Ruggero gave those very instructions, he took on all the expenses of the project and so we now have the promised *duomo*.

I see Iván go from side to side, walk away, come back in again, take photographs ... As a natural sceptic, he starts questioning the Norman origin of the building. But on observing the roof and its wooden construction, he can't suppress a whimper you could translate as 'unprecedented!'

'The arcade of the balustrade shows that the architect and the builders knew the art of vault making. Why didn't they use it when roofing the nave? It evidently needs more effort and time than a wooden construction, but there isn't a church in the entire Iberian Peninsula, however humble, which pays any attention to these arguments. Cathedrals with wooden roofs are found in England where stone is so scarce and wood so abundant that the choice is understandable. But in rocky Sicily they can't be short of quarries ...'

'There's something else,' observes Ro. 'Look at the capitals, those really uncouth stone figures, those human faces. Check out the enormous head, the mouth and the eyes open in such a horrible smile. It's no saint, more of a devil ... None too Christian, what do you reckon?'

'Well, there are many churches from Galicia to Germany,' adds Ka, 'adorned with similar figures on the outside and sometimes inside, eroded by time, but still sufficiently clear to see men, women, animals all entwined in sexual acts even a Hindu temple wouldn't dare to dream about: everything with anything, so much so you can't tell who's on top or underneath, let alone who's with who.'

'The official explanation is that such decoration shows the terrible deviations of hell,' concludes Iván. 'But the faces of the people, carved with those wide smiles, show something other than suffering.'

'So then, what's your conclusion?' I ask.

'Alright, I wouldn't be surprised if this cathedral was truly Norman.'

'*Mamma mia*,' so much chatter just to get here. I check my watch ... it's already gone five! Unless we get going immediately, we won't reach Bagheria before nightfall, one of the essential enclaves of Borges' Sicily. I hurry the others, who seem hypnotised by the enveloping charm of the town. They lean out over the viewing points, imbibe from the drinking fountains, hum to themselves strolling along the pavements ... Come on, Bagheria!

Ka assures me that I've got nothing to fear: Eureka hasn't melted and, if we drive at a good pace, we'll be there at the time we intended. I'm so tense and tired that once I take a seat it's not long before I fall into a deep sleep, my head barely has time to rest against the window.

Bagheria

WAKE UP, *BELLO*, we're here already.

It's Ka's voice; she has stepped on the accelerator to get to Bagheria before seven thirty, leaving an hour until Villa Palagonia closes to the public, at least according to the tourist information I've got. The villa forms the backdrop to a plethora of snaps from the little red book. I stretch out in the back seat, somewhat dazed but with the sensation of having slept more than a Rip van Winkle full of Lexatin.

We've still got a couple of hours of daylight left, and Bagheria, former playground of the rich from Palermo, doesn't seem too big. The first noble to build a mansion here was the Prince of Butera in the middle of the seventeenth century, who, when faced with the then Viceroy, found Bagheria to be an unbeatable corner to escape the little court. Other wealthy men followed, and the place didn't take long to become something akin to a luxurious housing development characterised by the most exquisite taste.

FULCO DI VERDURA, a relative of Lampedusa, visited these spots as a child, before emigrating to the United States where Coco Chanel would turn him into a highly prized designer. He left some very charming memories of his childhood, in which he describes in detail the life of this particular lost arcadia: 'Bagheria was roughly to Palermo, what Frascati was to Rome,' he wrote. 'A big borough dotted with gardens in which stood the sumptuous villas of the nobility. Some very, very grand like Valguarnera, Cattolica, Trabia, Butera, San Marco, Cutò; some smaller, all on one floor, with terraces and pavilions and, of course, the one and only Villa Palagonia with its monsters.'

Yes, we already know a bit about it, but where is the villa in question? The photographs lead you to believe that it must be a rather tranquil space, surrounded by nature. However, the town seen through Eureka's windows is a chaos of cars and mopeds roaring through the not exactly luxurious streets.

'Villa Palagonia ... they also call it the *Villa dei Mostri*,' my friends tell me. 'I think we ought to ask someone.'

So we do. Some passers-by are completely unaware of its existence; others have heard of it but don't know where to find it. Only a few dare to give us directions, and back and forth we go, until we're guided to an ugly roundabout. On one side there's a petrol station, on the other a stall selling roasted chickens, and further along ... at last Villa Palagonia! It would seem the old mansions of the aristocracy have been sidelined by the dirty and shapeless city, and even the Palagonia hasn't escaped this treatment. But it's unmistakable, with the two stone giants guarding the entrance ... and a wrought iron gate blocking the way, without Cerberus to open it for us.

'And now what?' asks Ro.

'There has to be another way in. Let's wander around and see.'

We circle the walls, topped by the celebrated monstrous statues that give the place its nickname. As there appears to be no alternative entrance, the situation is bordering on the distressing, like a sweet taken from the lips. We'll have to return to the main gate and try again. I don't even want to consider leaving it until tomorrow before visiting the villa. The others won't let us lose an entire day, however much I dig in my heels. I tell myself not to succumb to panic.

Through the railings of the gate a closed *biglietteria* can be seen where a sign refers to the entrance fees, and there it is – the main building. We see two black Mercedes parked next to it, and everything seems to indicate that the interior is inhabited, but by whom? Ro resorts to using an intercom listing the inhabitants' names next to its buttons. She presses at random, a certain Doctor Whatshisname ...

'Doctor Natale Tesdesco! Didn't he write a prologue for one of Sciascia's books, *Ore di Spagna* [*Spanish Hours*]? But he lives here?' I say perplexed, and press the bell again.

There's no answer. I try another. And as if by magic, without any reply, the electric mechanism opens the door for us. We hesitate a little before taking the first step.

'We're like four atheists slipping into heaven,' says Iván.

'Ladies and gentleman,' I comment in the tones of a tour guide, 'we're in the Villa Palagonia. Erected in 1705, it's no contradiction to say that it's one of Sicily's most fascinating corners. Between the walls, finished with sculptures of grotesque figures, the visitor is completely isolated from the outside traffic. The stone phantasmagorias loom over our heads with supernatural breath ...'

We all sense an approaching adventure. We open the little red book and read Borges' first comment: 'María,' he exclaims enthusiastically, 'we're going to a place visited by Goethe and Swinburne!'*

We're walking around a place visited by Goethe, Swinburne and Borges.

I read Scianna's text: 'Above a seat he finds a conch shell that he immediately puts to his ear to listen to the sound of the sea ...'

For me, this is the strangest photo of the series. The last thing you'd expect to find here would be such a shell, which leads me to suspect this casual find theory. I'd bet my Czech

*Borges confused the poet Algernon Charles Swinburne, who never visited the villa, with his great-uncle, Henry Swinburne, who wrote about it.

Bagheria, 1984: In Villa Palagonia

edition of *Fictions* that someone took the shell from a pocket and handed it to Borges, or that it was put there as a *fait accompli* in order to create the situation. The animal certainly didn't get there using its own footwork, yes a conch really does have a foot, only one, but a foot nonetheless.

I'm not fond of the Argentinean maestro's smile in this shot either. I've seen his smiles in other photographs, in television interviews, and they don't usually signify happiness. They're like a tic, with a touch of the chronic or senile about them, maybe even of courtesy as well. Borges launched into these smiles with the same ease they were wiped from his face, and neither option was a true reflection of his state of mind.

Let's now look at the shell, and the childish myth that they all contain the sound of the sea. No adult puts any faith in this experiment, which can be simply recreated by a concave hand or any hollow object of similar proportions. No, I doubt Borges was truly entertained by this joke. But let's go a bit further. Looking closely at the shell he's got in his hand, you can just see the cavity that malacologists call an *umbilicus* – at least the commission I had editing a guide on shells was useful for something! – and it's held in such a way that it's pointed away from the ear.

Eccola: Borges didn't even hear the message.

'The sea,' the maestro once said, 'is an old language that I haven't managed to decipher.'

Or perhaps he did indeed hear it, but only because he wanted to hear it. Because he, himself, was a kind of giant mollusc; in love with the ocean, with its resonances and infinite echoes, enclosed in his carapace, wound around the helicoidal staircase of his library as if it were the columella of a calcareous refuge. Because it's possible that the marine murmur of shells, like the fantasies of books, require a certain innocence from us, a little benevolent participation and, certainly, a great deal of desire.

Bagheria, 1984: In Villa Palagonia

We have discovered that the photographer Ferdinando Scianna is from Bagheria. Due to this being his hometown, it's not improbable that he proposed a trip around the Villa of the Monsters to Borges and María Kodama. Taking into consideration how the guest was a lover of the fantasy genre, and that he wrote a very elaborate *Book of Imaginary Beings* with his compatriot Bioy Casares, it's not difficult to believe that the idea was a dead cert: this place is full of them.

The above image shows Borges seated next to María Kodama on a baroque stone bench. His expression is jovial, his hands, as always, resting on the cane. He's wearing a dark suit jacket and black polished shoes. Behind him, in stone relief, an aristocrat is framed in a niche: periwigged or with long curly hair, a tepid poisonous smile, dressed in what appears to be a suit of armour.

I've consulted several texts on the Palagonia, but none are clear with any certainty about this person's identity. I tend to think that it's Don Ferdinando Gravina, the fifth prince of Palagonia, who conceived the construction of the villa. He handed the works to his trusted architect, Tommaso Maria Napoli, when Bagheria was still open countryside. If he lifted his head today and saw the turbulent *Scalextric* surrounding the place, he would, without doubt, remain as we see him, cold as marble.

The bench is easy to find: circling the main building in a clockwise direction, it's the first thing you see: we almost bump into it.

I guess Scianna feels a particular weakness for this corner of the villa. I know that he also photographed a local poet called Giacomo Giardina here, although I'm not sure whether it was before or after Borges. In this shot, despite María Kodama's playful caress of the statue, he appears as rigid and venerable as the supposed Prince of Palagonia. Giardina, on the other hand, looked out of the corner of his eye at the relief, with what, at first glance, seemed a sarcastic mistrust. He adopted a more comfortable pose, elegantly informal. I've also seen another photo of this same bench, one by Ferrante Ferranti. Replacing the poets, there is a little mongrel dog sleeping on the stone, with a muzzle fastened over its snout. A fine foil for the two aforementioned images: the poets like songbirds on one side, the gagged dog on the other.

I consult the little red book. Scianna says: 'Borges is fascinated by the history of the bizarre prince who peopled his villa with monstrous statues. He wanders among them reciting Swinburne's poems, "my mother's favourite poet", he clarifies ...'

Why Swinburne? I ask myself, and consider some possible answers: because the Englishman, who boasted about his blue blood, suits the villa? A more than acceptable hypothesis. Because his fame as a wretched blasphemer sits well with the profane atmosphere of this place? It's possible. Because Borges quoted Swinburne so compulsively, without it being relevant, just like I quote him? I plump for the last one.

I search for a poem of Swinburne's, among Borges' favourites, that isn't too out of place with the Villa of the Monsters. The Argentinean always highlighted the verses of *Laus Veneris*, full of joyful eroticism and no regrets, which he also considered untranslatable. I'm not going to be the one who contradicts him. This one's for you doña Leonor:

> Ah God, that love were as a flower or flame,
> That life were as the naming of a name,
> That death were not more pitiful than desire,
> That these things were not one thing and the same!

We're also intrigued by the bizarre story of the Prince of Palagonia. What impulse, we wonder, prompted him to scandalise his neighbours and guests with this formidable collection of gnomes and giants, serpents, voluptuous nymphs, dragons, and even musicians, who, although camouflaged, are not out of tune in the bestiary. They say there were around six hundred in total, although many have been lost forever, leaving sad gaps along the wall; their complete demolition was once requested by the locals, as they felt threatened by the old Eastern superstition according to which pregnant women who see a monster are destined to give birth to monstrous children.

'I don't think they're so hair-raising,' says Ro. 'Rather than statues, they're like puppets, don't you reckon? It's like being Alice in Wonderland here.'

'I think the prince must have felt very lonely, and he put up this lot in order to invent some company,' adds Iván. 'Look how the sculptures *look inwards*. They don't seem designed to create an impression from beyond the walls, at least these ones don't. They aren't a *cave canem*.'*

'Don't discard the notion that other figures also existed which looked outward, maybe with time they've been lost,' I add. 'But you're right though. They're not frightening, more like guests at a well-attended, but rather silent party.'

While the others stroll around the garden and take photos, I slip off to take a seat in the exact spot where Borges posed. I close my eyes and concentrate to try and reconstruct how much the maestro could have perceived in his day. The first thing is the cold of the stone on the buttocks.

❧

I suggest the same game to the others; something business executives would usually call brainstorming. Or in this case, a storm of sensorial impressions. Let's start with the olfactory:

'A strong smell of oleander, everywhere,' says one.

'It seems like jasmine to me,' argues another.

'Conifers,' I add trying to mediate. 'It smells of pine and summer picnics.'

'And at the entrance,' we all conclude, 'a dense odour from a *panineria* and a roast chicken stall. It must have made Borges hungry.'

---

* *Cave canem* is Latin for 'beware of the dog' and famously appears on a mosaic at the entrance to the House of the Tragic Poet in Pompeii.

Bagheria, 1984: Visit to the Villa of Monsters

We do the same thing with our auditory faculties:

'An ambulance siren screaming.'

'Agile piano notes gently wafting down from an apartment.'

'The meow of an incarcerated cat.'

'The gravel crunching under foot.'

'The explanations of Scianna, and the voice of María Kodama, I'm sure, affectionately accompanying the sighs of the old man.'

I take note of all this as we pass on to another image from the book: Borges side-on, standing out against one of the garden walls supporting the monsters. A prickly pear juts into shot on the left. A wild shrub sprouts from the wall, along with various electricity leads. You can also see an entrance arch, dark like a tunnel.

Starting to take an inventory, I double-check the image for the creatures I'm able to distinguish: a more or less human figure in the lower section, above some relief scroll work; a jumble of dragons; another, possibly female, humanoid at the apex of the arch, placed above a large smiling head. It's not easy to recognise them, because the camera lens has tilted and they appear blurred. Where are they?

We retrace our footsteps to start again. The entrance, as we subsequently find out, wasn't the original access point, but a modern urban addition created for that purpose. At this precise moment two locals appear through a door, two good-natured elderly men. We decide to ask them:

'Excuse us, do you know where to find these figures?' and I show them the image from the little book.

One of them carefully examines the picture, twists his head from side to side and reckons we should turn the corner to the right, or round the central building to the left by some 240 degrees, if we want to prolong the excitement. In a nutshell, we have to face the garden wall where the sun goes down.

'*Tante grazie*,' we say.

'Spagna?' the guy asks us.

'Yes.'

'*Viva España*! Down with Franco!' he proclaims, fist in the air, in perfect fiery Spanish, and walks off smiling.

Here's the sought after corner. The prickly pear has disappeared, replaced by a coquettish shrub. The wild rocket on the wall has also been wiped out, and the cables changed for a new installation. The only unaltered feature is the family of monsters. We hesitate a while before confirming our find, but the layout, and above all one definitive detail – a decoration projecting from the right shoulder of the central figure – are enough of a guarantee.

I'm not sure if Borges would have realised, but long before the building of Villa Palagonia, in 1552, the equally titled Prince Vicino Orsini ordered the architect Pirro Ligorio to construct the Bomarzo Gardens, another zoo of petrified monsters. They say many of them are still standing in his villa at Viterbo, very close to Rome, and, of course, in the pages of the most celebrated novel of Borges' fellow Argentinean Manuel Mújica Láinez, one of his old friends.

Later I discovered via Joachim Fest that these Gravinian eccentricities also inspired many German authors: Arnim, Wieland, Heine, Stifter … However, whilst we're talking of Germans, they horrified Goethe, who defined the Palagonia as a 'tunnel of dementia' and interpreted it as a 'premonition of *sick* romanticism'.

'His Werther really was sick,' mutters Ka, possessed by sympathy towards *our* Gravina. 'Due to him, half of Europe was shooting itself in the head every time a woman said "no".'

Sick, or should one say mad. Ferdinando Gravina is the model of a wealthy yet unhinged man, a literary figure straight out of Cervantes or Shakespeare. If rich men weren't mad, so says the Sicilian proverb, the poor man wouldn't be able to live. But for our prince it isn't just any old madness, or, as Hamlet would say, it seems there is method in the madness. It's a heretical madness, a subversion of the established order. Sciascia must have asked himself something similar: 'How is it that, while the rest of the world turned towards grace and charm, the Prince of Palagonia turned to horror? Was it a premonition, a penitence, a perversion?' And his friend Savatteri sketches out an answer: 'It was all of these things. But one ought to remember that only a part of humanity *turned to grace and charm*, while the majority remained stuck in the abyss of work, pain and injustice. Gravina, even from his aristocratic viewpoint, from his Sicily, from his villa in Bagheria, must have been a sure witness to this. A man like him, oppressed by titles and fame, couldn't openly rebel against the customs, the laws, the rules. Perhaps he didn't want to. However, he *felt* the need to profess his heresy, his own immense mistrust of man and God. How to do this without risk? Transforming blasphemy into madness'. In Sicily, as we already know, all roads lead to Pirandello, for whom acting wildly was neither more nor less than confessing the truth face to face with a neighbour.

I also have increasing doubts about the Prince of Palagonia's supposed madness, and this inclination to think of his monstrosities as an act of rebelliousness against Reason, against the idea of a garden as an instrument to order and control the landscape. The dreams of Reason, as we know, are a tireless generator of monsters. You would need a well-furnished mind to be able to create such a topsy-turvy world, and to know those around you well enough to determine exactly how you could scandalise them. I bet if Ferdinando Gravina had been a young aristocrat in the twenty-first century, he would wear heavy metal band T-shirts and spiked wristbands, or something similar, so he could create an impression on his neighbours.

I stay alone with Ro to take some snaps, when we're surprised by a somewhat dishevelled local woman in a visibly bad mood, who has come out to let her children play in the open air. She asks us what we're doing, and I would be exaggerating if I claimed that my dreadful Italian was up to the task of explaining that we only want to take a couple of photos.

'The villa is closed, it's closed,' she repeats. 'Without a ticket you can't stay here. This is private property.'

'OK, we'll go,' I promise her.

However, we've still got to find another Borges photo in Bagheria, and we can't leave without discovering it – so call the cops or even the army! Quietly, we pretend to walk towards the exit and, like sneak thieves, turn back.

⁓

Only now do I see that if someone had wished to raise a palace in honour of a Borgesian universe, it would have been difficult to conceive of anything more successful than Villa Palagonia. Added to the fantastical and monstrous legion surrounding it, there is also a real Hall of Mirrors. This must have surely delighted the maestro.

To enter we have to go up the main staircase, to the side of the aforementioned bench with the stone relief of the prince. The hall is usually closed outside opening hours, but luckily there is a wedding party getting immortalised on film inside. Newlyweds, bridesmaids and photographers all look at us with a certain amazement. Our scruffy appearance gives us away; bermudas and sarongs, unshaved guys and girls with tousled hair, salt crystallised on arms and legs. However, when we confidently congratulate them they refrain from blocking our way.

According to Joachim Fest, the original furniture was taken out so that tourists could enter. Already knowing Ferdinando Gravina, anything was possible when it came to designing interiors: '... the old chairs with clawed feet of unequal length or spikes on the seat, or those on which it was only possible to sit facing backwards, or the twisted tables, or the vases made from fragments of porcelain china and broken chamber pots ...'

The entrance hall, to all intents and purposes, is completely cleared except for some painted murals. It leads on one side to the private rooms of the prince, and on the other to the Hall of Mirrors. Above the entrance there is an inscription, which I note down:

Bagheria, 1984: In the Hall of Mirrors of Villa Palagonia

Specchiati in quelli cristalli e nell'istessa
magnificenza sincolar contempla di fralezza
mortal l'immago espressa

Ro translates for me: 'See your reflection in the glass and contemplate in its magnificent splendour the image of mortal fragility that it expresses'. So it seems the little prince had a black sense of humour worth considering. We don't lose heart and prepare to check our own mortal fragility, still dressed as fancy-dress shipwreck victims.

We're alone, the whole room to ourselves. From the walls various busts, blind and anonymous, spy on us. They're sculptured from marble and another translucent material, set into as many niches decorated with shells, arabesques, curved mouldings, pure rococo delirium. The ceiling, lightly arched, breaks into a painted frieze imitating an over-elaborate lattice in greys, golds and sky blues. It even has the appropriately blooming flowerpots. The rest is a collection of blackened sheets, quicksilver faded with time, but still struggling to multiply our image when we lift our gaze towards it.

It's possible that Pirandello, who was from Agrigento, was also thinking of this hall of mirrors when he wrote, more metaphorically, the following: 'when a man lives, he lives and does not see himself. Well, put a mirror before him and make him see himself in the act of living, under the sway of his passions: either he remains astonished and dumbfounded at his own appearance, or else he turns away his eyes so as not to see himself, or else in disgust he spits at his image, or again clinches his fist to break it ...'

Although Pirandello is most well-known for his *Six Characters in Search of an Author*, his creation of theatre within theatre, the average reader misses one of his principal contributions, so present in his stories and novels: the idea of life itself being theatre. This theatricality is presented as a psychological mechanism related to a game of mirrors. There is a conflict between being on stage and in the stalls, or as Sciascia certainly said, between living and seeing yourself live. It would seem the Prince of Palagonia was a specialist in this.

'The dream of some kind of narcissist,' says Ro looking at the ceiling.

'Yes, what your average adolescent wouldn't give to have a ceiling like this at home, before going out on a Saturday night!' jokes Ka.

'Maybe Borges didn't see the mirrors. Maybe the mirrors didn't see him either,' murmurs Iván enigmatically.

I think I know what he means. Something in the room doesn't fit. I go back over some lines I've scribbled ... Did I write *our image*? No, it isn't exactly like that, the effect seems still more startling. If I look above, or for that matter vertically, I can't make out my reflection, but I see that of my friends.

A strange game: I see everyone except myself.

'It's odd how Goethe, such an omniscient, omnipresent and all-embracing narrator if ever there were one, was so disgusted by this place,' I say again to Ro.

'Because he was omniembittered,' Ka retorts.

'The good thing about the mirror is that it allows us to recognise ourselves, to know what we are,' I get pedantic. 'Like many people, from childhood Borges was scared by the possibility that a reflection would show a frightening image or just emptiness, as with vampires or certain infinitely small elements of particle physics. I reckon the most perverse thing is the way in which it reflects what we don't want to know about ourselves.'

I LOOK FOR THE MAESTRO, that is to say, the corner where he was photographed. The image was taken from below, a fragment of the ceiling clearly visible. Definitively, the panel behind him corresponds to the entrance. It's as if the writer had just entered, taken a few paces towards the centre and stopped. Then, he turns his head to the large windows spilling abundant light over the floor, and ... *flash!*

Now I turn to Scianna: 'In the Hall of Mirrors [Borges] can't help but remain speechless in front of the mysterious play of reflections, so important in his work. However, I'm not referring to his recitations or his verses, but to the unknown expressionist poet who, in one of his sonnets, imagined a room where the walls, floor and ceiling were uniquely made of mirrors in which his image was reflected to infinity ...'

He may be right, that this room doesn't recall our ephemeral condition, but quite the contrary: the ability to be many *selves,* even through the artifice of dirty glass, until we run the risk of becoming conceited, until we believe in an immortal infinity. And I think that the Argentinean maestro, aside from childhood terrors, may have measured the monstrosity of this object we call a mirror by just such a possibility, by the many chances we have to continue existing, to challenge oblivion and death, if they're not the same thing, using similar tricks; in other words by emulating their divine omnipresence and inescapable visibility.

Now I fear the mirror may disclose
The true, unvarnished visage of my soul,
Bruised by shadows, black and blue with guilt-
The face God sees, that men perhaps see too.

'The eye with which I see God,' I once again demand my turn to be no less mysterious than Iván, 'is the same eye God uses to see me.' This is what Eckhart used to say, a German mystic who Borges would have been perfectly happy sharing a few drinks with until the light of dawn.

'You're starting to talk nonsense,' advises Ka.

'You mean if we look in these cloudy mirrors, God will see us in turn as the poor blemishes we are,' replies Iván, courteously following the long-winded discussion.

'Wipe those blemishes and the slate clean,' the girls order us to shut up. 'We ought to get going.'

Ferdinando Gravina, Prince of Palagonia, lives on in his house; Borges, thanks to the medium of photography, is his life-long guest of honour. We leave, yes, but with the grateful sensation of having spent the afternoon in such exquisite company, and the happy suspicion that something of us will also remain, captured forever, in the heart of Villa Palagonia.

Ficarazzi

THE PROXIMITY OF PALERMO, already a magical city in my memory, is noticeable as soon as you leave Bagheria. We feel how it pulls us, with its magnetic power. I believe in the magnetism of capital cities with the dust of centuries over their domes, with abundant cultural layers in their subsoil. I believe in the gravitational force they impose on their surroundings, covering a fairly extensive radius, and in their ability to scatter invisible yet urgent enticements through the air.

Owing to mistakes and a lack of funds, however, tonight we'll stay on the outskirts, like an impatient battle encampment waiting to take the much-desired citadel at the break of day.

WENDING OUR WAY rather aimlessly, with the continuous cover of night stretching over Eureka's bodywork, we pull in at a little village called Ficarazzi: a settlement true to the fisherman's orthodoxy of narrow streets, scarcely illuminated at this hour. From their frayed beach seats at the entrance to their houses, the women look at us with surprise. Tourism can't be too common in this village, as I realise it doesn't often feature in the guides I've read. The children, no less surprised, dart around or press their bicycles towards the car like a school of dolphins signalling a cheerful welcome.

Meanwhile, Iván is once again suffering at the wheel.

We're circling through a labyrinth, not exactly Borgesian, half covered in tarmac and without any signs to guide us.

'I think we've already been through here.'

'No, we can't have, we came along a street parallel to this ...'

'We can't turn here, try the next one ...'

'Turn left, let's see ...'

In such a pandemonium of identical whitewashed corners, it was simply a matter of time before we came to a halt in a street without an exit: desperate, the headlights of Eureka fall on to an unyielding wall. We try to reverse, but the narrowness of the road, the cars parked cheek by jowl on both sides and half the children of Ficarazzi playing around us, make the manoeuvre a demandingly reckless exercise.

Ariadne, where are you when we need you? I inwardly say to myself, and seconds later my prayers are answered. Coming towards us are a brigade of capable housewives resolved to rescue us from the breach.

'My niece can help you, she drives around here every day,' one of them assures us.

To our great surprise the candidate to relieve Iván from his position at the wheel is a pregnant woman of at least eight and a half months, judging from the excessive size of her belly. Our friend resists in order to maintain his pride, but in the end gives up his seat to this pregnant fairy godmother in whom we have no other choice but to place our faith.

'Come on, Iván, it's no disgrace,' we console him with sadistic humour.

'*Tranquillità, Non ti preoccupare: é pilota di formula uno,*' one of the other neighbours confidently assures us.

The choice was a good one: blessed be the fruit of the womb that, at the height of gestation, got into the front seat to save Eureka. With energetic and millimetric turns of the wheel, pedal pushing and gear changes, she put us back on the road, leaving behind a trail of effusive thank yous and audible sighs of relief.

Having learnt our lesson, we decide not to abandon the coastline under any circumstances, a direction that never fails. Luck leads us to a beach scattered with empty loungers. We park our car next to a line of mopeds, double-checking out of the corner of our eyes the groups of youths drifting around the area. It's not that we've got much to steal, just that we've filled our quota of shocks for the day.

Nearby, there are two large marquees, similar to fairground stalls, illuminated by two psychedelic floodlights and shaken by cacophonies of sound from that subtle instrument of torture known as Karaoke:

'*Gloriaaaa ... chiesa di campagna, acqua nel deserto, lascio aperto il cuore, scappa senza far rumore, dal lavoro del tuo letto, dai gradini di un'altare, ti aspetto Gloriaaaaaaa ...*' a frustrated wannabe pop star bleats away, some two hundred metres from us, all for the redundant glory of Umberto Tozzi.

We sit on the loungers and, on a towel, spread out the food we bought on leaving Bagheria: the still hot roast chicken and the watermelon, both promising to taste glorious. The meal passes in happy harmony, still joking about Eureka's mishap and the providential intervention of our pregnant Ariadne.

Having collected up the leftovers, Iván and I search the surroundings for a better place to spend the night, preferably away from the excess of the discos. We climb some rocks abundantly covered in slime and, on the other side, discover a cove that, at first site, appears safe and discreet.

We spread out our blankets and sleeping bags, the temperature and humidity seem reasonably tolerable. It's not long before we slump down exhausted. Plump stars shine, just like a planetarium, in a completely cloudless sky. Then the Mediterranean starts to whisper a song from the cradle, or so it seems: a flamenco lullaby sung in time to the low and rocky rhythm of the shore.

Palermo

AGGRESSIVE EARLY-RISING LAWRENCIAN rays drag me from a long, dreamless sleep. On the other side of the rocks, a growing murmur alerts us to the continuous arrival of bathers on the neighbouring beach. We remain protected by the natural screen, but we don't know for how long. Ro is still asleep next to me. A few metres away, Ka is stretching. I look at the empty sand of the cove noticeably dirty in the daylight, blackened by the ashes of old fires.

'Whereabouts is Iván?' I ask.

'He's gone for a dip,' answers Ka.

I gaze again towards the metallic blue of the waters and can make out his blonde head, bobbing up and down with fish-like pretensions.

'I'll go one better,' I proclaim. 'I'm going to swim *naked.*'

'Iván *is naked*,' Ka informs me.

On the shore I strip off my trunks and immerse myself in the sea. The low temperature immediately activates my blood flow like an injection of caffeine. I stumble on the submerged stones, upholstered with moss; they feel somewhat disagreeable to the touch of my feet, and I launch forward without thinking. I swim out to Iván with the wonderful sensation of floating in amniotic fluid, enjoying the way our nakedness is deformed and illuminated by the light dancing on the surface.

Ka swims over to keep us company. I opt to leave them alone and return to terra firma. Lounging on my sleeping bag,

I scribble some anarchic notes while I half look at Ro as she gets up, arches her back, stretching out in a feline way. Silently, she moves to the seashore and deposits her clothes. Although Sandro Botticelli had a weakness for blonde Venuses, he wouldn't have turned down the model now before me.

Urbanites as we are, it seems a true luxury to feel like carefree Robinson Crusoes, returned, even for a while, to our natural state, determined followers of the Lord of the Flies – which are already starting to buzz in the hot air. Refreshed, we collect up the camp and cross the thin stony line separating our intimate bay from the Sunday uproar. We dodge towels, sand castles and ball games in order to load Eureka's boot and drive, at last, to the island's capital: Palermo awaits!

Palermo has so many memorable echoes for me; I have a great many fond expectations. The heat is on the rise and the deluge of light beating down on the city makes me smile as we enter via the marina of La Cala, bristling with masts.

'All these poles ... they look like lances, what do you reckon?' comments Ro, her hand feeling along the seat for mine, until she squeezes it. 'It's like a live version of the *Surrender at Breda*.'

We pass by the small and flirtatious Politeama Theatre, and further on the other grand Palermitan theatre, the Massimo, the masterwork of Giovanni Battista Basile and his son Ernesto. We greet the colossal lions that guard the impressive entrance stairway day and night, as well as the ghost of Coppola's daughter who still seems to be fading away, so badly, in the final scene of Godfather III.

'Yes, just like everyone else, I reckon it's the worst instalment of the saga. What went wrong? I'm not sure. The script was good; the cast, except for the insipid Sophia, was worthy of the occasion; there were some potent images ...'

'Al Pacino said it was a mistake to try and redeem Michael Corleone,' comments Ka. 'Perhaps the director forced this plot line too much, and all the epic poetry of the story collapsed.'

Maybe that's true, but I didn't feel so disappointed by this. I feel it had a certain tragic grandeur, a Shakespearian touch. Thinking about it, Borges would have liked the idea of the death on the steps of the Massimo, convinced as he was that humanity is forever condemned to repeat the story of Caesar's death at the hands of Brutus. Coppola's variation, the death of Caesar's daughter, far from distorting the story, accentuates its effect: eradicate the seed, end the race.

'Don't forget Michael Corleone also had a son,' Ka corrects me.

'He'd already put an end to his part: he became an opera singer,' I reply. 'And look at the ending of the story, as well as Shakespearian and Borgesian, it's also Pirandellian. Everything happens at the doors of a theatre, after the performance. The curtain falls outside as well as inside the coliseum, it's inspired!'

'You're going to end up deciding the third part is the best,' adds Ro.

LEAVING ASIDE SUCH CONTROVERSIES about the silver screen, we plunge headlong into Palermo. As with Rome's *quadratta* street pattern, the heart of the city is a criss-cross of two perpendicular avenues, Via Maqueda and Corso Vittorio Emanuele, called the Quattro Canti: four very Vivaldian concave corners, with allegorical representations of the four seasons. The traffic is constant, as is the bustle of pedestrians. At least at this time of the morning, Palermo feels like a living city.

We leave Eureka very near to this spot, in a parking lot watched over by the young Giuseppe. He's a teenager of about fifteen, with slicked-back hair, wisps of a moustache and the air of a little Mafioso in the making.

'Don't worry,' he tells us hitting his chest. 'Giuseppe will take care of your car.'

We hand over the keys and watch him manoeuvre Eureka with the virtuosity of a pregnant woman from Ficarazzi. I'm sure he isn't old enough to get a license, but his eyes sparkle with life, artfulness, and so much self-esteem that he even talks about himself in the third person. Who knows, great cinema careers are also built from nothing.

Our first obligatory stop is Santa Maria del' Ammiraglio or La Martorana to friends. A fantastic Norman church – Iván has no doubts this time – with a profusion of Byzantine mosaics. It sheltered plotters from the Sicilian nobility who handed the island's crown to Pedro II, the Aragonese. The only plotters this morning are wedding guests attending a Greek Orthodox ceremony, which doesn't stop us from admiring the magnificent craftsmanship of the walls and the spirituality they exude. It's enough to give one a desire to pray, if it wasn't for the fact that we've forgotten all our prayers.

However, for mystical ecstasy you'd be better off going to the church of San Cataldo, a few steps from La Martorana, but without any effusive ornament. In fact, today it appears to be open just for us. The floor has its original mosaic, and numerous restorations have managed to keep the blind arcades, small windows and pink cupolas looking like they were finished yesterday. The souls of brave templar warriors still seem to float through these spaces. The church lends itself to the proposal of an innovative principle of physics, according to which the condensed silence is capable of elevating us.

Thus purified, we approach the church of San Francesco, but only to honour Jorge Guillén, the Spanish poet most valued by Borges, who wrote a long poem inspired by this very corner. I fear things have changed a lot since then, but that doesn't stop me enjoying the unhurried rhythm of his verses, which start rather poorly but fortunately soon begin to really pick up.

Gothic, but not too emphatic.
The piazza, the artisan, and the morning,
sonorously, make the scene.

A donkey has to pull
a little cart full of fruit and vegetables,
with gaily decorated trappings.
The brilliant colours of a ribbon
add the finishing touches to his head.
The strong willed ass brays.
Donkey no! A mule now
passes by, brushing its request.
Think in contrast of Polyphemus,
who truly voiced his worries. Sun of Sicily!
The clear air envelops the murmurs
that continue in accompaniment.
The Medieval Age is here,
so silent from its façade.
The grapes, the tomato – with their greens,
their reds – and that luxurious purple
of the aubergine
They shine, they tempt
under such light,
the same sun of Ages.*

There aren't many donkeys now, but a whole lot of murmurs and sunshine, and yet more sunshine. We're walking back towards the Quattro Canti when we come across the University. Did they receive Borges here? If, indeed, they did and if

---

* Translator's Note: Here is the Spanish original of this hitherto untranslated poem by Jorge Guillén: '*Gótico nada enfático./ La plaza, menestral, y la mañana,/ sonora, suman pueblo./ De un carrito de frutas y legumbres/ debe tirar un asno,/ los carros joviales./ Vivísimos colores de una moña/ concluyen la cabeza./ Rebuzna el asno con deseo fuerte./ ¡Borrica no! Ya un mulo/ pasa, roza la súplica./ Se piensa por contraste en Polifemo:/ canto bien su ansiedad. ¡Sol de Sicilia!/ El aire claro envuelve los rumores/ que, sucesivos, van acompañándose./ Asiste la Edad Media,/ tan silenciosa desde su fachada./ Las uvas, el tomate –con sus verdes,/ sus rojos- y ese lujo de morados/ en la gran berenjena/ resplandecen, seducen/ bajo esta luz de ahora,/ el mismo sol de las edades.*'

we were to find some conclusive clue, it would be an excellent addition to my pursuer's notebook. In his prologue, Scianna spoke of a ceremony at Palermo University in which thousands of young people came 'to acclaim him and hear him speak about the metaphor. They cried "Long Live Borges!" With his usual decency, the maestro relied on modesty: "This is the result of a combination of overly generous circumstances. A few years ago, I had the chance to analyse such an occasion, trying to understand the enthusiasm of students in Texas. The fact is I'm Argentinean, I'm old and I'm blind. The Argentinean was always a colourful personality, looked upon favourably. An old blind poet like Milton or even Homer is easily treated with respect. My work has nothing to do with this. If I was deaf, for example, it would be different. Deafness has no poetic aura."'

We cross the threshold and skirt a courtyard baked by the sun. Some students are exchanging notes, others are consulting grades and dates on a glazed noticeboard.

'Law. It's the Law Faculty,' I sigh, deceived.

The last place I would have wanted to find myself in Palermo, the place which reminds me of the course I still have to finish, since who knows when, in order to complete my degree in this loathsome subject.

'I should have guessed when I noticed the smell of judges' wigs, robes and sulphur. Guys, if you don't mind I'll wait for you outside,' and I leave to light a cigarette.

We turn into Vittorio Emanuele. On both sides of the street, various bargain bookshops display their wares to the public. There are heaps of junk, yellowing bestsellers and self-help manuals, but also cut-price editions from the local publishing house Ed.bi.si, whose Sicilian themes – Goethe, Maupassant, Pirandello ... – and modest ochre covers captivate me. I leaf through a few examples and then separate from the others so I can peek into the Regional Library. Its interior, totally modernised, is an icy aluminium, poorly related to the world of wood, dust and silverfish I had imagined.

Such disappointment is frequent not only in Sicily, but in almost the entire Western world. It makes me think of the Italian architect Alessandro Mendini, who used to criticise design as 'a progressive artificialisation of the natural'. The keepers of historic buildings direct all their efforts towards maintaining the external appearance, guaranteeing that the tourist doesn't leave without a photo. Almost always, the interiors are another thing altogether: either just ignorant, or overly audacious restorations with a misguided sense of modernity or pragmatism; if not improvised, hurriedly designed or with a manifest bad taste.

Similar thoughts are not far from our mind when, later on, we visit the cathedral. From the wide square enclosed by a balustrade sprinkled with statues, all the way up to the slender towers of the southern façade, the exterior has a contained but definite beauty, at times, calling to mind the bubbling gothic of Majorca or Seville. Even the arch joined to the bishop's residence has its own singular charm. Initially a Byzantine place of worship, then a mosque and later a Norman church, it was finally disfigured by the Neapolitan Bourbons. It's to them that we owe this naked and indecisive interior, incapable of moving us one iota. As an additional punishment, visitors wearing sleeveless shirts are required to cover their shoulders with some sort of clothing so as not to offend the saints. Lacking such items, you have to pay thirty cents on the door for a paper parallelepiped (worth the alliteration), rather similar to the disposable tablecloths they use in Cádiz bars.

Various old women in mourning are praying in the pews. A pair of altar boys cross the central nave with a demeanour that is less holy than conniving.

'There's nothing to see here,' says Iván.

We pass through the Porta Nuova with all due caution, as a great deal of traffic also rushes through this spot. I have a drawing to hand, I think by the Abbot of Saint-Non, showing the same gate crowned with flags, and crowds of people on the balconies of the loggia and as many in the street, among drapery and platforms, ready to witness a grand parade. The arch, which is trying to be Greek, or perhaps Roman, has greatly deteriorated due to earthquakes. These days, judging by what can be seen, it's held up by four stone Atlases known as the Moors due to their turbans and moustaches. The upper roof, covered in tiles, glitters beautifully in the midday sun.

A few soft drinks help us to pass the time until La Cuba, the famous Norman palace, opens to the public. Iván wants to track down a few more historical footprints; I just want to say that I've visited one of the settings for the *Decameron*, otherwise known as *Prince Galahalt*, Boccaccio's masterwork.

In the story, some young Sicilians kidnap a girl from another Mediterranean island, Ischia. After much discussion as to who should have her for himself, they resolve to present her to King Frederick who

> ... commanded that until he was feeling stronger she should be lodged in a very fine pavilion attached to a garden of his that he called La Cuba, and looked after there ...

Poor girl, I think as I enter the grounds, having paid two euros to see the four rather sad walls still remaining from the twelfth century. Even the cupola that gives the place its name hasn't been preserved. And what about the lavish gardens? Perhaps it's better not to mention these: I know chalets in Conil that seem like the orchards of Versailles in comparison.

'At the very least they could've confined the girl in Cuba, capital of the Caribbean Antilles, she would've had a much better time in captivity amongst daiquiris, mulattos and coconut palms,' I sigh.

While I'm getting bored stiff – in keeping with the vegetation surrounding me – Iván is completely fascinated by a vast Arabic inscription, carved in stone, which is displayed in a nearby room. He spends a quarter of an hour taking notes and scratching his head when Ro, who also has a smattering of Arabic, comes to his aid. Another fifteen or twenty minutes go by, but it seems like a hundred.

'Have you deciphered anything?' I ask them before we go.

'Not a word,' they answer acting naturally. 'No doubt it's made up.'

I have no arguments to combat them, but there is evidence that Muslim Palermo was one of the great capitals of the Mediterranean. More reliable historians think the city had 300,000 inhabitants and up to 500 mosques, of which not one remains standing. The writer Tariq Ali, in his novel *A Sultan in Palermo*, recreates the splendour that was only comparable to the Caliphate of Córdoba. The arrival of the Normans didn't break this apart; on the contrary, they integrated with Arabs, Jews and Greeks, adopting the habits of the former, surrounding their churches with gardens whilst promoting the arts and philosophy at their court. However, I fear the passage of time hasn't left much of Moorish Sicily, except a few names, a formidable agricultural tradition and a liking for spices in the island's cooking.

Just in case the boredom, heat and schlepping around end up finishing me off, it might be an idea to stay close to the cemetery; Palermo's is small, but crowded. Once inside, we look for the tomb of Giovanni Tomasi di Lampedusa, author of that cornerstone of Sicilian literature known as *The Leopard*. Our on duty cinema buff, Ka, mentions the greatly acclaimed film based on the book, which, for many farfetched reasons, I've never managed to see. In any case, I fear Burt Lancaster and Claudia Cardinale, under the direction of Visconti, would exaggerate the decadent splendour of the leading family, which is paradoxically the least interesting part of the book for me. After travelling around the island for a while, I find it difficult to believe that Sicilians would have easily recognised themselves in such rich and affected characters. In order to make the work their own, to see a common identity in the emblem of *The Leopard,* I think they must have looked further into the story, lingering on the thousands of details slipped in between the lines: the atavistic ideas about death, the notions of sin, the fleeting nature of love ('flames for a year, ashes for thirty ...'), the attitude to resignation and sorrow ('those quick wits which in Sicily usurp the name of intelligence'). There is also a certain pride transformed into blindness, the politics of changing everything so that nothing changes; history as a wretched chess game in which the invaders always win – the outlet for an unprecedented popular indifference towards the flag ruling over them – not forgetting the often cited dialogue between the prince and Chevalley about Sicilians' dreams. These nuances are too subtle and transcendental to catch at twenty-four frames a second. I believe that a populace, and people as individuals, are frequently defined by what they desire. In *The Leopard* there are more wishes than reality, and this could be the strongest link between the book and its readers.

Is there something more? This seems like a reduction, a nonsense. By rereading the pages of Lampedusa, I start to think that the prince wanted more than just to reveal the decadence that now makes dandified second-rate poets and petulant ersatz little leopards tremble with emotion. The book also extends an exasperated appeal for self-criticism, an urgent call to escape from underdevelopment and vulgarity, to be aware of solutions, possible prospects and capabilities. From the perspective of childhood nostalgia and love for his homeland, Lampedusa rallies against the Risorgimento, against the regrettable flow of the island's history, but also against the provincialism that neutralised any form of progress. He ignored the fact that all the feudal lords decisively contributed to such fateful backwardness, that they made robbery a characteristic trait of the island.

In his long novel, *The Viceroys,* Federico De Roberto tackled the same aspect of Sicilian reality, but he knew how to see it from the other side, the viewpoint of the serfs, the eternal losers. However, he was negatively judged by the pope of Italian critics, Benedetto Croce, and his importance waned.

Lampedusa, albeit posthumously, had infinitely better luck. Undoubtedly, his no less ferocious way of grabbing us by the lapels isn't to everyone's liking. But what is the secret of such unanimous applause? Francesco Orlando, disciple and friend of the author, has his own view: 'I tend to smile when realising how Lampedusa's present fame is seen as a reason for regional pride by our Sicilian compatriots, or rather as he would say, is seen as a new pretext for obtuse pride. And I ask myself if it's great art or, simply, the printed word which manages to take the sting from the more bitingly severe judgments, making them painless.'

In conclusion, everybody loves Lampedusa because he's famous, and they see in this celebrity a reflection of their own greatness – also because they haven't read him, or, rather, they have their own reading of the book, a reading that serves as an alibi to justify everything. I've known many writers who have been victims of the same infamy: ignored during their lifetime, if not actually scorned, until one day they gain a certain recognition – usually from a foreign source – and the masses put them on a pedestal where they can see themselves represented. Borges knew something of this. In any case, I'm pleased to know that the author of *The Leopard* is still carrying on the fight from the depths: his genius revived, ever more caustic and pointed, every time one of his books is opened and that marvellously penetrating light shines out.

I'M NOT SURE if the pleasure of strolling around a cemetery lies in its testament to our own temporary nature, automatically stripping us of so much banal and everyday anguish, or if it's because we're aware of ourselves above and not below the ground. Borges, who has a couple of beautiful poems dedicated to the gravestones from La Recoleta in Buenos Aires, never left us his opinion either, but one of his obsessions concerned these fateful dates carved in marble. He saw a ferocious simplification of human life between these two sets of numerical symbols.

In this Palermo cemetery, the eloquence of the numbers becomes horrifying. Some families have buried three, even four sons, without any reaching twenty. More than a few marble plaques have photos of the deceased. Standing before them, the visitor is unable to conceive such an abundance of pain; he prefers not to know the causes that so filled the Grim Reaper's schedule. And at the same time, he better understands the resigned veneration of death practiced by the Sicilians. Death: if you can't beat it, join it, they must have said whilst experiencing one of the particularly abysmal low points in their history.

The same questions relate to everyone, those laid to rest in niches and those whose bones are housed in luxurious pantheons, wider, and without doubt more economical than many flats in Madrid's Lavapiés district. What became of the Stagnos, the Virgas, the Falcones? Did the lives of the Arezzos, the Ruvolos, the Spasimos have meaning? Did the Piazzas, the Collisanis, the Lo Monacos, the Bonfantis, the Cordones atone for their sins? For the rich and poor, for the honest and the criminal, there is also just one answer: the silence of the cypresses, the mute movement of the cats.

Knowing that Lampedusa was a full-blown prince, we're sure his remains must, at the very least, lie in a family vault similar to the others, whose names have been chiselled deeply enough to ensure that time won't erase the tribute too soon. This assumption considerably lengthens our search until we give up and have to ask the guard.

'Oh, yes, Lampedusa!' he gabbles with a toothpick between his lips. 'Third row on the left.'

But we find nothing, not a trace of the writer. Wait a

moment. What if he wasn't buried in a vault? We look among the ordinary tombs, at ground level, and immediately come across the grave: a modest portion of earth, enclosed by a little wrought iron grill. The austere stone with his name and that of his wife, Alessandra Wolff-Stommersee, the Lithuanian psychoanalysis-loving baroness, who was so decisive in encouraging her husband's literary vocation.

AS IF WE HADN'T HAD ENOUGH ludicrous folly for one day, we've got an even gloomier place to visit: the Capuchin crypt, famous for being home to more than 800 bodies in differing states of preservation. They say that rich Palermitani used to pay considerable sums to subject their dead selves to the mummification procedure thought up by the monks: letting themselves be dried in a cave, away from humidity, and then be exposed to the sun. Dressed in their Sunday best, they were classified by sex, age and status, and then lined up as part of the macabre gallery to entertain morbid tourists for all eternity.

At the entrance, a monk straight from central casting for *The Name of the Rose* religiously collects donations whilst selling postcards and exhaustive full-colour catalogues. For a very modest price, one can take home the whole deceased army.

Once inside the cellar in question, the atmosphere becomes unbreathable, partly because of the silent spectacle before us and partly due to the massive flow of people. Everyone who enters here gets a similar impression: in certain corners, the skulls are piled up with their sockets pointing towards the visitor. Looking for Yorik amongst this lot would be like searching for the proverbial needle in the haystack.

Some mummies are now little more than a messily dressed-up ossuary, and others are trying out impossible expressions, grimaces that seem to rebel against their inevitable rigidity. One of the star attractions in the collection is a very small girl enclosed in her coffin, a deeply moving sight. She appears to be sleeping, still vulnerable, helpless.

> ... And a small step separates the two
> worlds, never were life and death so
> united and joined in friendship.

So said the poet Pindemonte. The whitewashed walls and metal structures do nothing but reinforce the sensationalist, and powerfully Dostoyevskian, effect of the setting.

'What was the intention behind all this?' asks Ka, noticeably horrified.

'To feed the Sicilian's morbid side,' suggests Ro, who is victim to similar worries. 'And to remember where we're all eventually headed, like the medieval thinkers who had skulls on their writing desks.'

'A huge *momento mori*,' I agree.

'I see their aesthetic side,' adds Iván, stirring up a debate. 'Do you remember that exhibition we saw in London? Gunther von Hagens, the German surgeon who patented a revolutionary technique for preserving cadavers, and showed figures of humans and animals in different poses. They were dissected in such a way they appeared to be anatomical studies, like you see in textbooks, or like those jigsaw puzzle models used by medical students.'

'Absolutely, he unleashed an enormous controversy about the moral limits of art and the right to dignity in death. All because the figures were displayed playing football, riding horses or in some such type of pose, and the public found it humiliating.'

'Taking one example, nobody remembered the Egyptian mummies in the British Museum,' says Ro.

'Or the deceased in the Capuchin crypt,' puts in Ka. 'In the end, maybe what links one with the other is the desire to spend the rest of eternity like this. They have agreed to be museum pieces rather than dissolving into nothing.'

It's not that this trip through the house of the dead has made us hungry exactly, but it's gone four and we've gone all day without a bite to eat … Furthermore, we've still got a lot of Borges to trace in Palermo. Iván and Ka decide to go on the hunt for some *focaccia*, while Ro and I head for the Palazzo dei Normanni.

WHEN YOU LEAVE THE BEATEN TRACK in Palermo, in other words, when you move away from the sites of historic and artistic interest, you're assailed by two immediate impressions: one is the feeling of being in any street of any town anywhere in the world; then you look a little closer and the other becomes apparent: being able to identify Sicily's capital by its large amount of scaffolding. There is no corner of this planet that competes with Palermo in shored up building façades. I can see dozens of beautiful structures on the point of ruin, centennial stone trembling on its foundations. If this were Africa or South America, perhaps it would be more understandable, as their priorities are different. But Sicily is Italy, and Italy part of the European Union, which has offered important funds for years precisely so this doesn't happen. Someone told me that much of this aid has periodically been *diverted* by the Mafia. Evidently, if until very recently these people couldn't or didn't know how to stop the flow of human blood, how were they ever going to be worried by their architectural heritage?

Palermo, the 'perplexed city'. So said Lucio Piccolo, the metaphysical poet who introduced Lampedusa to the literary world. Roberto Andò, from the Palermitan cinema scene, collaborator of Francesco Rossi, Fellini and Coppola, returned to his home town fascinated by following Piccolo's footsteps. This led to a deeply felt yet very bitter diary of his experiences, where the debris, the perplexed debris of Palermo, is mingled with the moral collapse of its inhabitants. 'I was born and grew up in a dead city. I can say such an atrocious thing because a city – Palermo in this case – has

Palermo, 1984: In the Palazzo dei Normanni

the possibility of becoming what it was born to be, that is, a pause in time, even when physically the things which make it up, the houses, streets, the monumental echo of its past, the balance between what could be lost and the brightness of the future, are falling to pieces like bones, whitewash and plaster.'

Well, at least the Palazzo dei Normanni is still standing, undefeated. Like so many other buildings we've visited, the gigantic fortress has been the object of countless changes – as many as the hands that have held its reins of government. Various extensions and building works abandoned over time explain its irregular shape. The city's first settlement was established right where the building now sits, in Piazza Vittoria. The Arabs built on top of the Punic and Roman ruins, then the Normans made their additions – four towers, of which only one survives, the proud Pisana tower – and later on the Spanish Viceroys used it as their residence. Today, it houses the Regional Assembly, and is also one of the most visited tourist attractions.

I open my little red book. I see Borges in his venerable old age, seated in an armchair with a leather back. The strangely young hand, free from supporting his weight, this time rests absent-mindedly on the cane, without the pressure created by the need to maintain his balance. His clothing remains the same as in previous photos, but now the light seems to confer a certain healthiness to the octogenarian's face. Under his sagging eyelids, even his pupils, squinting in their irreversible blindness, appear to shine with more life. The position of his head, tilted upwards, makes his hair look longer. Behind him there are numerous volumes with illegible titles lined up in a bookcase. The spines on the upper shelf, uniformly worked in gold leaf, suggest an encyclopaedia. The lower shelf, with a matt finish, could be from a more limited series.

The simple composition, as it deals with the Argentinean, is in perfect harmony. He is, and always will be, irrevocably associated with books, even more so than any other writer.

He lived in such close proximity to them that he almost seemed to be made of leather, paper and thread, rather than flesh and bone.

We ask a guard if he recognises the room. He looks intently at the photograph, clicks his tongue and says to us:

'It's here, in the Palazzo dei Normanni.'

A round of applause for the quick-witted public servant. But where exactly? Is there a library here? Another minute of careful observation, a shake of the head, a new click of the tongue:

'I don't know, it could be any office or study. Anyway, no tourist is allowed to enter any of them.'

Our first disappointment; ignoring the discouragement, we return to the task.

I quickly look for the other image, the one in which María Kodama holds out her hand to embrace Borges. They both smile with spontaneous happiness. As with the shot in the Hall of Mirrors, Scianna crouched down so he could include the ceiling of the room from below, which is blurred by the effect of the focus. Although tricky to see, one can make out something akin to a metope, but not the markings or drawings contained within.

'And this place, do you know it?'

'Ah, this one yes,' says the guard. 'It's the Hercules room of the Regional Parliament. But you can only visit on Monday, Thursday and Saturday mornings, and it's essential to book in advance.'

'But we're leaving tomorrow and ...'

'That's provided the Assembly isn't in session,' he adds, as if he hadn't heard us. 'I'm sorry, there's nothing I can do.'

Unsuccessful, tired and hungry, we sit down on the stairs of the palace. I look again at the last photo. The setting is the least of it. Two people who love each other, laughing together. What could they be saying? Could they be enjoying some erudite and ironic remark, of which Borges was a

Palermo, 1984: With María Kodama in the Palazzo dei Normanni

tireless fount? Or could they be pretending to govern Sicily as king and queen? In the middle of pondering this Ro makes me jump:

'Wait! Those details at the back, I'm sure I've seen them passing by a kiosk selling postcards ... It's in the palace, but I think we should look in the Palatine Chapel, let's go and check.'

Whether it is or not, we go up to the first floor and tour around until we find the desired chapel. We join the queue, as they only allow in a limited number of tourists, but it's not long before we can enter. Inside, in addition to the usual prohibitions, no photographs or video, they also require silence, I guess so as not to disturb the fundamentally spiritual atmosphere of the place.

Straight away, I realise that the courtyards, staircases, rooms, in fact the entire Palazzo dei Normanni appears to be a wrapping, as solid as it is delicate, for the Palatine Chapel, the heart of the building. 'A plaything therefore, a jewel of a basilica' in the opinion of Maupassant, but with the merit of having a floor with three naves in a much reduced space, which we hardly have time to contemplate. 'The most surprising religious jewel dreamed up by human thought', also according to the French traveller and writer, is a colourist explosion full of gilding that seems to radiate light, with a spectacular panelled ceiling decorated with Eastern motifs. The honeycomb cells, alveoli or stalactites are indeed dazzling, as are the biblical scenes in every nook of the architectural structure.

The multi-coloured mosaics gazing down from above are also beautiful. In reality everything has an overwhelming visual impact, which makes me wonder if Borges was able to enjoy even a fraction of the concentration of delights denied to his eyes. Then Ro points out the main apse, with the large figure of Christ the Redeemer accompanied by an inscription in Greek characters that she kindly translates:

I am the light of the sun, he who follows me
will not walk in shadows, and will have light in
his life.

I try to imagine Borges, such a well-known expert in shadows, with a smile on his lips after hearing this solemn warning. And speaking of sunlight, a guard beckons us towards it immediately as a new consignment of tourists await their turn to enter.

On leaving I see a dark and fleeting blur out of the corner of my eye. It's a cat; a strange presence in a palace like this. By a simple association of ideas, I think of Beppo, Borges' cat. In reality he was called Pepo, but when the maestro heard the name they say he didn't hesitate in rechristening him after Lord Byron, and he was so fond of him that he even dedicated a poem to the animal. When Borges visited Sicily, his silent friend had already been dead for a couple of years. So it's amusing to think that this other feline, black as night, could be something akin to a shady reincarnation, a negative of the celibate white cat of those verses.

I look at him for a while: he doesn't let himself be scared off by strangers, though he keeps a wary distance. I approach slowly, once by his side I stroke the smooth fur on the back of his neck as I recite to him:

> Your back allows the tentative caress
> my hand extends. And you have condescended,
> since that eternity, by now forgotten,
> to take love from a flattering human hand.
> You live in another time, lord of your realm-
> a world as closed and separate as a dream.

'Shoo!' blurts out Ro. 'Don't go wasting the afternoon on cat poems. It's already gone five thirty.'

She's right, we haven't got time to lose. We get going in pursuit of the next step on our search. But before we leave I take a photo of this black Beppo, wondering what would happen if the printed picture reveals nothing but the cold architecture of the Palazzo dei Normanni.

Our energy levels are waning and the time is flying past, so we decide it's best to take a bus to Piazza Marina. Once there, next to the Garibaldi Gardens, the Palazzo Chiaramonte (also called the Palazzo Steri) opens up before us.

The bellicose, scheming Chiaramonte family were considered the de facto rulers of the whole island for years and were obsessed with maintaining their privileges. They instigated the building's construction and traditionally lived in its apartments, until a great-grandchild of the patriarch Manfredi was beheaded in this very entrance by Martin I of Aragon.

It wasn't the only blood spilt in the palace. The building used to house the headquarters of the Holy Office and heretics were placed in its cells. In his work *Death of the Inquisitor*, Leonardo Sciascia has this description: '... this palace was a fortress within the city – no less overpowering than their

Palermo 1984: In the Palazzo Steri

castle at Racalmuto and all the others they scattered across Sicily ...'

It's hard to shake the feelings brought on by knowing that the Steri was previously the scene of atrocities perpetrated in the name of Christ. Even the alterations, designed by the architect Carlo Scarpa, to convert the palace into what are now the university offices, don't appear to have completely renounced this cruel past. As an example, the system of gridded bars keeps the interiors in gloomy shade, though they're well lit today and full of bureaucratic languor. Little is left of everything else: the sandstone walls, the agonised graffiti written by the accused, the painted wooden ceiling, the sixteenth-century exterior staircase much spoken of by the building's admirers – they remain closed to visitors or simply consigned to memory. Perhaps to lost memories.

Ro reminds me that it was scarcely a couple of years ago when the Pope asked for forgiveness, in a poor and tardy manner, for the Inquisition's crimes. It's decades since I practiced as a Catholic, more than once the temptation of apostasy has crossed my mind. I remain defeated by laziness as, no doubt, I would have to confront a panoply of bureaucratic obstacles put in my way by the bishopric. However, I can't help being saddened by the excesses of finding a way through such a system, by these modern versions of hunting and persecuting heretics, witches or anathemas. Without belonging to it, I would prefer the world I live in to have a more conciliatory and less obscurantist church.

A breath of evening breeze brings me these terribly beautiful verses of the maestro's, from the sonnet where he lends his voice to an inquisitor:

> ... I have forgotten those who groan,
> But I know that this despicable remorse
> Is a crime that I add to the other crime
> And that both must be swept by the winds
> Of time, which is longer than the sin
> And the contrition. I have wasted them both.

We have come, I haven't forgotten, in search of Borges. His serious, circumspect face has an empty gaze fixed somewhere in the middle distance. He stands out against a diffuse background, like a softened charcoal sketch, in which the observer thinks he can recognise a column and two twisted palm fronds.

We enter the central patio. Undoubtedly, Scianna took the portrait here. The unmistakable columns are projected into semi-circular arches constructed with solid blocks. Where the arches converge, some little carved heads can just be made out. The plants are definitely conspicuous by their absence. In their place a cement mixer and sackfuls of earth clearly indicate the place is undergoing restoration. An employee approaches to inform us of that very fact and asks us to be brief, something that is becoming all too common.

I quickly take a few notes and photographs, consider I've got it covered and reopen the little red book.

This other image must also come from the courtyard in the Palazzo Steri. It shows Borges with María Kodama in front. He is facing towards the left of the photo, her eyes looking towards the right. She is attractively turned out, with her first white hairs, her lips wanting to break into a smile and a slight timidity in her countenance. Two red roses are clasped to her chest, which owing to the light possess a strange mineral brilliance.

As I've already mentioned, when in Palermo Borges received a golden rose weighing around half a kilo in recognition of his achievements. It was much more expensive and heavier than the flower of his beloved Coleridge, which the poet imagined receiving in a dream as proof of having been in paradise, and on waking found in his hand: a beautiful metaphor for the old idea that all writers, even scribes like myself, are part of the infinite poem that is the whole of literature.

The maestro's work is full of roses – what one could call a rosebush – and as in this work, they can appear as a symbol of the unattainable:

The Rose,
the unfading rose beyond my verse-
rose that's full and fragrant,
rose of the black garden in the deep of night,
rose of any garden and any night,
rose that's born again by the art of alchemy
out of tenuous ash,
rose of the Persians and Ariosto,
rose that's always by itself,
rose that's always the rose of roses,
the young platonic flower,
the blind and burning rose beyond my verse,
unattainable rose.

The rose that Paracelsus could throw on the embers of the fire and make rise from the ashes. The poets' eternal rose, the

Palermo 1984: With María Kodama

profound rose, the written rose, the rose that names with each of its letters all the roses in the world:

> ... Destiny allows me
> The privilege of choosing, this first time,
> That silent flower, the very final rose
> That Milton held before his face, but could
> Not see. O rose, vermilion or yellow
> Or white, from some obliterated garden,
> Your past existence magically lasts
> And glows forever in this poetry,
> Gold or blood-covered, ivory or shadowed,
> As once in Milton's hands, invisible rose.

'I have always wanted a rose to survive oblivion,' the maestro once said, surely picking up on his old idea that the immortality of one man is in the salvation of all men. The roses in María Kodama's hand, destined to wither quickly, live on in luxuriant health in the photograph.

'Or even longer in the case of the Golden Rose, unless it ends up in a foundry,' I add.

'Don't you mean a foundation,' Ro corrects me, wickedly.

'Are you sure I've not forgotten any of the medals they gave me?' Scianna remembers Borges saying while they were packing his cases. 'No, you're not missing any,' María reassured him.

Thinking about it, Ro and I don't have too many snaps featuring the both of us. When we've travelled together, we've always taken it in turns posing in this or that location, while the other takes the shot. On very few occasions do we have an amateur Scianna uniting us indelibly in a photo frame. If someone had appeared from behind a column and taken the snap this afternoon, I fear the result would have looked similar to the maestro and Kodama: with me looking to one side, and Ro, tired of my Borgesian persecution, looking to the other. But without a rose.

⁓

The Regional Museum, between Via Roma and Via Cavour, consists of three floors in what was once the abbey for Philippine monks. I imagine Borges crossing the street amongst cars and priests, inhaling the aroma from the *panineria* opposite or dodging, by ear, the ball being kicked at full pelt against the wall by a group of children.

It's as if I can see it all now, the maestro dressed in a light jacket, white shirt and dark tie with diagonal stripes. The badge and fountain pen still in place. Ro and I are sure that beige suits him much more than the funereal colour of previous days: it's a much better match for such a sunny afternoon and it takes years off him.

Safe from tomorrow's *calcio* stars, Borges – with us in his wake – crosses the first patio, then the next, and starts to move through the ground floor rooms. Scianna enlightens us: 'For him Sicily is Magna Grecia. He wants to see what is left of that world and that era'.

On the sixth floor, which is filled with the Casuccini

Palermo, 1984: The Regional Museum

collection of Etruscan artefacts, he stops before a funerary statue. A woman with wavy hair, covered by a cap decorated with geometric patterns. According to a note at the base, it dates from the second half of the sixth century BC. There are signs of former colouring, now almost completely faded. It was sculpted to house ashes: something approximating a bright emerald, monumental cremation urn.

With faltering steps or perhaps ceremonious respect, Borges advances – with us in tow – over the chequered floor. Some friezes with drawings of human figures are distinguishable in the background. They urge him to touch the lady on her throne. The writer puts his trembling fingers on the left hand of the statue, the hand holding a symbolic object.

Maybe he asks himself, 'Will there be a better fate than turning to ash, leading to oblivion?' as we, ourselves, also ask. I encourage Ro to do the same, to touch the figure. She doesn't need to rush at it; it's enough to brush it gently, like Borges. Just enough so I can photograph her without the guards noticing our desecration and bundling us out of the building. She manages to do it with the tips of her fingers. As the distance has to be so close, the glow of the flash will obliterate all the statue's details, fusing the stone hand to Ro's. I wonder if she has felt anything special. Perhaps something Borges could have also felt.

She looks at me, seriously worried at the decline in my mental health. Then she shrugs her shoulders and smiles.

∽

The stairs take us to the deserted first floor corridor, dedicated to Greece and Rome. The extensive collection of figurines, pots and ornamental pieces trapped behind glass becomes monotonous, at least boring to the layman. And what's more for the layman, given the time of day, we still haven't eaten.

The exhibited objects, gathered in such a manner, blur into one: it seems impossible, and surely useless, to stop in front of everyone. It amounts to invisibility by concurrence. Borges doesn't appear to recognise this effect. According to Scianna, he's like a kid in a sweet shop and isn't scared of admitting it: 'Look, María, look!'

This time I search for a smaller sculpture in blackened bronze. It's a Roman reproduction from the first century BC. It represents a Hercules subduing a stag, which in its day adorned a fountain in Pompeii and was a donation from the Bourbon King Francis I. The image from the little red book captures the moment when Borges touches, this time more emphatically, the demigod's thigh; the demigod with a monstrous nature, according to the Neo-Platonist account, spread by Borges himself. If I remember correctly, one of his famous twelve labours was to trap, alive, an Arcadian stag with golden antlers. Hercules' arms firmly hold the animal's horns immobilising its neck, while the divine knee presses down on its hindquarters to stop it springing up.

'Poor animal,' says Ro, but I'm not sure if she means the stag or the strongman.

Hercules never was top of my list. In contrast to Odysseus, who constantly showed cunning and intuition, he relies on force; his muscles are his only means of surprise. I'm also

Palermo, 1984: The Regional Museum

well aware that Hercules is a very familiar figure to me. As the mythical founder of Cádiz, he presides over the city's coat of arms with its two proud lions as bodyguards, along with the inevitable legend *non plus ultra* curled around the columns: the very wording which has, alas, caused such damage in the hands of chauvinists. We used to draw the crest at school when I was a youngster. The most difficult bit to do was the lions, and more than once I could have done with some help from the local statute passed by the Sicilian town of Canicattì with regard to their shield: 'This dog is a lion, according to decree number 34256, July 2nd 1925.'

When I got to the famous motto I used to think that it was far from certain there was anything further beyond. The world, as Iván often says, is made round so that you go round in circles.

Speaking of going round in circles, there's no time to lose: we must move on to the next objective.

Another photograph, one of my favourites. Once again Borges is abusing his position as an illustrious guest by handling whatever sculpture is put within reach. However, on this occasion his hand gesture is different. He isn't groping around in hope, as we do when lost in the dark. The palm of his hand gently rests on the cold face of Caesar, a Tiberian copy from 44 BC (sorry Iván), as if he's caressing him.

We bump into his carved form, so to speak, when turning the corner, halfway between the two ends of the gallery.

'He's handsome,' observes Ro.

The sonnet Borges dedicated to Caesar comes to mind and perhaps he recited it silently to himself while he touched the lifeless features:

> Here lies that which the daggers left behind.
> Here lies that wretched thing, a dead man
> who was known as Caesar. The blades have

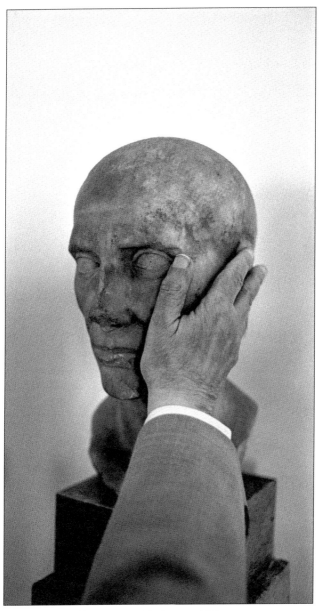

Palermo, 1984: The Regional Museum

opened craters in the flesh.
Here is the atrocious thing, here the
imprisoned machine once used for glory,
for the writing and execution of history
and for the sheer enjoyment of life ...

The statue's shaven head, boxer's broken nose, dimpled chin, parted lips, and eyes looking into the beyond as Baudelaire would say. He still exudes an authority I can't quite place. After all, you could say that he was the first president of a united Italy, not to mention Western Europe?

Here also lies the other Caesar, the one to come
whose great shadow will be the entire world ...

There's always a Caesar thirsty for power, as the Sicilians well know, and a bewitched knife ready to destroy his career. But nobody learns: even after Napoleon and Hitler, a new leader who's prepared to invade Russia in winter will invariably appear. We leave the world's lord and master where it most befits him, encased in his own statue, and carry on as we are, mortal and plebeian.

~~~

It occurs to me that the invisibility by concurrence found in the museum could also apply to the globe. I wonder if Sicily hasn't frequently been invisible in this world, if it hasn't been stretched to breaking point between so many fluctuating imperial powers. Much later on I read something about the island written by Fest and it makes me pause for thought: 'In contrast to Rome, Florence or Venice, in spite of its burden of historical traces, it seems curiously devoid of history. One only comes across vestiges of the past, a chaotic catalogue of stage sets that the imagination hardly manages to bring to life. The fact is that deep down the island lacks history; it has always been limited to being a setting, a mirror reflecting the power struggles of neighbouring regions and the rise and fall of empires. As soon

Palermo, 1984: The Regional Museum

as an image disappeared, the mirror's surface was emptied, and another image took the place of the former ...'

The German has reached a terrible conclusion, which has found its way into the collective consciousness and in some way manifests itself in the Regional Museum: he who has too much history, ends up having none.

End of the hunt, we must go. Our attention is wandering and our appetites aren't going to put up with any more delays, or we'll be fainting down the stairs. We go down to the colonnaded courtyard and are on our way out to the exit when I'm suddenly overcome by a strong feeling.

'I've passed here before. No, wait, this passageway ... Yes, it's exactly the same as ... Wait, that ...' and I open my little book, my missal with red covers, as Ro looks on dazed. 'This is it, it's right here! Yes!'

The image shows María Kodama and Borges walking away into the distance over the very same tiles. At the precise moment we near the spot, we see a group of noisy children leaving. Where a scaffold once stood to restore the garden area – you can see wooden boards used as little bridges and shadowy iron bars striking the ground – hedges and ferns now spring forth. Thanks to the stains on the columns, we know that Scianna stationed himself at this end, let the pair move forward until almost disappearing, and then clicked the shutter.

Although nobody is going to photograph us, I ask Ro to take my arm. She to the left and I to the right, just like the picture. We walk slowly. I close my eyes. I'm not sorry to leave behind the abstract semidarkness of centuries, the swell of remote voices fading little by little at each step we take; instead we have the pleasure of re-joining the hustle and bustle, in the common light of the here and now.

⁓

Our Borgesian collection only lacks two corners of Palermo. According to the little red book, both are found in a place called Villa Igiea, the precise whereabouts of which we have not the faintest idea. We look at the position of the sun and reckon that in a little over two hours it'll be dark. We need to hurry.

The first, and no less urgent, item is to head for the nearest hostelry and devour our weight in *focaccia*, our favourite energy booster. The second is to meet up with Iván and Ka at the prearranged rendezvous time in the parking lot of our friend Giuseppe, who has kept his promise and faithfully looked after Eureka. The third is to ask the way.

'Oh, yes, Villa Igiea,' answers the sixth or seventh person we've stopped in the street. '*Ma é lontano ...*'

Luckily, the rest has been good for our Fiat Punto and she wheels along at speed down the Via del Mare, leaving central Palermo behind for the higher parts of the city. It's obviously a prohibitively expensive area for modest pockets: grand mansions and fancy cars everywhere. However, we keep on going without any sign of the Villa Igiea.

'Guys, I've found it!' Ka informs us after a while spent going round in circles, during which we suffer from a growing inferiority complex.

Palermo, 1984: In the Basile room of Villa Igiea

It's a hotel. Villa Igiea is a hotel, surely the one that played host to Borges during his stay in Palermo, with five stars above the door, no doubt. There's nothing for it, we have to see it.

'Looking like this, we won't last five minutes before they chuck us out on the street,' fears Iván.

'I'm not so sure,' I reply. 'It's easier to get thrown out of some grimy billiard hall than a place like this. The receptionists never know if you're the nephew of a European monarch or a simple snooper with a Borgesian fetish. You, yourself, could pass as a descendent of the Russian tsars.' I flatter him in order to raise his self-esteem in the hope that it will aid his ability to deceive. 'If you think about it, they'll be very cautious of throwing us out in such a way. You can bet on it.'

My little talk has the desired effect, but we carry on without being too convinced. We hesitate outside for a few minutes, until a young couple dressed in bathing clothes enter and provide us with a bit of temporary cover. We position ourselves behind them and, while they ask for their key, I hurriedly search for the photo of Borges in Scianna's missal.

'Excuse me, we're looking for this room, Salone Basile ...' and I show her the image.

If needed, I'm prepared to swear that the man in the photo is my great-grandfather and that I want to pay a brief tribute to him, but it won't be necessary to stoop so low. The girl on reception, very polite and smiling, not only recognises the room straight away, but also takes us to it herself. She even has the kindness to close the door, allowing us to stay as long as we want.

'At heart the working classes suffer from a complex that stops them feeling comfortable in these kinds of places,' I explain to Iván en route. 'It's not economic differences which separate us most from the rich, but a certain way the rich have of not letting themselves be impressed, even of hiding it when they really are impressed. If you invite a beggar to a posh do, he'll feel overwhelmed by the quantity of dishes and, owing to damned modesty, will end up asking for the cheapest thing on the menu.'

'You win,' my friend surrenders. 'Let's play at being rich.'

We explore the room with Ernesto Basile's name, the Palermo architect who was commissioned by the powerful Florios to construct the hotel and design part of the interior in a very refined Art Nouveau style, including six suites to which, I fear, we're not going to get easy access. Such is life: this poor man's baroque, the modernist aestheticism verging on Deco, now adorns the wealthiest places. The pamphlet given to us by the receptionist states that Villa Igiea has a lecture hall, sea water swimming pool and tennis courts, as well as an endless list of other services.

As soon as we enter the room, off to the right, I recognise the table where Borges was seated when the photo was taken. It's still in the same place, along with the three fluidly designed chairs, allowing me to set them out in the same way as Scianna. The huge carpet, which was already rather well used, has been removed, revealing parquet flooring in an excellent state of repair. The old white curtains have also been replaced by new ones, with a floral pattern. Everything else remains intact: the basket-handle arches, the doors, the heavily ornamented walls, the splendid lamp, the mirrors! The most recent decorators have added the odd flowerpot in a corner; I guess they revive the room's atmosphere.

Ro takes her revenge and gets me to sit in the chair where Borges presumably sat. After a playful struggle I give up and adopt the same rigid posture in front of the camera as the writer, which in my case is motivated by modesty.

'So, what are you feeling?'

'The desire not to move until breakfast time,' I answer.

Sauntering along the hallways as if we owned the place, we dare to go for the Igiea prize as the hotel's worst dressed inhabitants. Among the photographs of illustrious guests displayed on the walls, we recognise a really young King Juan Carlos, the very picture of happiness. And why wouldn't he be, amongst such luxury? Returning to our previous topic, I've always found it strange the way backpackers scorn comfort, as if the only valid way to see the world was via sacrifice and austerity. I greatly respect the kind of travellers who, despite having few resources, throw themselves into an adventure, but who also know how to enjoy luxury if it's at hand. A journey doesn't necessarily have to be an exercise in masochism, in the same way that true love doesn't have to be a story of penury and suffering. And, if as Iván usually says, the real journey is inside oneself, I doubt the soul has such a vocation for discomfort or, for that matter, sybaritism, as does the body.

We go out on to the terrace and admire the entire bay of Palermo and its dazzling blue. We stroll around the small labyrinth of hedges, which we rather kindly refer to as a miniature version of *The Garden of Forking Paths*.

The damp path zigzagged like those of my childhood.

Palermo, 1984: In the Villa Igiea

Indeed, Borges must have enjoyed this, just like a child. Very near to here, there's an area offering therapeutic massages for only one hundred euros. Now we better understand the relaxed expression on Juan Carlos' face.

LUCK ONCE AGAIN presents us with another Borgesian corner, the last one of the day. When we lean on the balustrade overlooking the bay, I notice the stone spheres adorning it. In one of Scianna's photos you can see their reflection, along with the sea and mountains, in the glass behind which the maestro is posing, seated and searching for the sun with his rigid eyes. The glass in question is behind us, and somewhat given away by a triangular sticker, in place so people don't break their noses if the surface is extremely clean. The sticker is now a logo in modernist characters, easily read the wrong way round, saying Villa Igiea. The round-backed chairs from the dining room are no longer there either: today's are square and appear to be less comfortable. The solitary palm has definitely aged well, and is still growing in the same soil next to a few newer companions.

I read Scianna's comments: 'I find Borges on the hotel terrace, in front of a limpid sea. The day is beautiful. The Spring, which has been so capricious this year, even in Sicily, seems to have made an exception for him. He looks like he's savouring the intoxicatingly subtle perfume of the air. He says that he feels the sky must be a perfect blue, he turns towards the sun, ignoring the light but not the heat, and starts to recite: "Sweet hue of Eastern sapphire ..." before pinpointing with a timid smile: "Dante, Purgatory, first canto". He goes on to quote others, from D'Annunzio, Marino, always on the theme of the sky's colour. His way of paying homage to the country receiving him is to quote verses from its poets'.

Before leaving with a heavy heart, Iván and I look for the toilets accessible to the public. I'm sure Borges' friends know a veritable battery of anecdotes about accompanying him on trips to the bathroom and pointing him in the direction of the porcelain, moments when his proverbial intelligence and sense of humour must have shone through.

I imagine myself accompanying the maestro to Villa Igiea's toilets. In order to get there you have to go down some ancient wooden stairs, which Borges, apprehensively, would have heard creaking. He would have also noticed the thick carpets at the entrance and enjoyed the delightful smell of the soap, which even differs between posh hotels and the grotty guesthouses we've all known.

'Mission accomplished, girls,' we announce with the map open. 'We ought to tell you that the Igiea has no rooms free. No, I'm afraid they won't let us sleep in the garden. So we've got to find somewhere, the same or better, to spend the night. What do you reckon to the Sferracavallo campsite?'

Mondello, Sferracavallo

IT'S GROWING DARK as Eureka slips along the road towards Cape Gallo. Beautifully changeable views are offered up before us: small quays, coves and copses, as coquettish headlights slowly come on with the sinking reds of sunset.

It's almost dark when we arrive in Mondello, seen as Palermo's real beach. It's heavy with terraces and showy neon pubs, that wouldn't be out of place in the night-time skyline of the Spanish Costa del Sol, with its yacht jetties and lively seaside strollers. In his memoir, Fulco di Verdura referred to Mondello as a paradise, but by the seventies had already recognised that the place had degenerated a lot from the arcadia of his childhood. Today it's a town of frivolous, empty, perhaps even fraudulent, idleness, as if painted or drawn on papier-mâché, but it's also enjoyable, even ideal for giving the senses a rest, and why not?

The day has been a full one, we all feel happy and affectionate. However, when Iván and Ka kiss in the middle of the street, we hear some unmistakably disapproving coughs.

'Italy, land of *amore?*' says Iván laughingly. 'With all the similarities between Sicily and Andalucía, the countryside, the affability of the people, the way they pat each other on the back and chat, there's a fundamental difference. Have you noticed that nobody kisses in the street? Not in Messina, or Syracuse, or Palermo ... "To make love you should head for the South?" Not the South of Italy, that's for sure ...'

'Any moment now we'll see a sign with crossed lips saying *È vietato darsi baci ...*' bets Ka.

'You'll be pleased to know that Lampedusa also criticised Palermo's puritanism. "There's no city where one fucks less", he once told his friend Francesco Orlando. Maybe the prince is exaggerating a bit, but he certainly has a point.'

We take a seat at a random pizzeria and, never more aptly, pay dearly for the innocent mistake of asking for a salad that isn't on the menu. A mediocre pizza for four, bread, water, cover charge and service – which they religiously collect in Italy – costs us thirty seven painful euros.

'They fleece you more in Mondello than Golgotha,' Iván protests. 'Let's get out of here as soon as possible.'

'Not without a game of table football,' I challenge him. 'I saw some amusements on the way over here.'

In the games hall, between billiard tables and space invaders, Ka and I take on Ro and Iván. Although I'm no table football virtuoso, I've played enough to be confident we'll win. After a thrilling duel, we're defeated in a closely fought contest by four goals to three. Naturally competitive, I surprise myself by taking defeat happily – testament to how content I feel on this trip. The passions aroused by football – shared so fervently by Sicilians, Spanish and Argentineans – albeit, in this case, the miniature version, haven't affected our happy mood of enjoyment.

'We're delighted that you haven't got a quote from Borges to illustrate this debacle,' the victors say to me.

'I'm only going to say what a spontaneous passer-by once shouted when he crossed paths with the maestro: "Borges and Maradona forever!"'

Eureka is off again, Ro dozes on my shoulder as we drive along the darkened road from Mondello to Sferracavallo, a small rather lost coastal town where we intend to spend the night at a campsite. This time we overdo the precautions to avoid getting led astray, although the town is so tiny this isn't likely. We rent a bungalow and try to get comfortable, if we can, in bunks worthy of the worst military barracks.

Segesta, Trapani, Erice, Marsala, Marinella

AFTER A MORNING SHOWER, we breakfast in a small Sferracavallo café called La Delizia, just like that hotel in Adrogué where Borges once intended to kill himself. The assistant, a living portrait of my deceased grandmother Mami, dries her hands on her flowery apron and waits for our order with a big maternal smile. Her excellent cappuccino is enough to justify the name of the establishment; it's a shame she only has three cups, which forces us to take it in promiscuously rotating turns.

Whilst waiting for his, Iván entertains himself by translating the poems in Sicilian decorating the walls, the majority rather overblown compliments to the locality. By reading them you notice that the locals call their town Sferracavaddu, due to the phonetic mutation distinguishing their island dialect from peninsular Italian. The name means *Unshodhorses*, certainly an abrupt place name, which doesn't do justice to this attractive corner of Palermo coastline.

WHILE RO CHATS to the owner of the locale, I begin to regret the little contact we've had with the inhabitants of the island until now. Indeed, it's very difficult to really understand the soul of this land, but are the Sicilians themselves accessible? What traits do they have in common? Do they correspond to any profile? The portraits that others have outlined since antiquity are diffuse and generally somewhat harsh, namely the following:

Cicero: 'Intelligent and suspicious people, born for controversy'.

D. H. Lawrence: 'The Sicilians simply don't have any subjective idea of themselves or any souls'.

Scipio Di Castro: 'Their character is made up of two extremes, because they are extremely timid and extremely foolhardy'.

Gesualdo Bufalino: 'They ought to have their DNA changed'.

Giuseppe Tomasi di Lampedusa: 'They think themselves perfect; their vanity is stronger than their misery ... Lock five Sicilians and five Piedmontese in a room to solve a problem. After a quarter of an hour all the Sicilians and none of the Piedmontese will have an answer in their heads. But after an hour all the Piedmontese and none of the Sicilians will have solved the problem'.

Giovanni Maria Cecchi: 'Haughty, unless there is a big difference in social status, they do not give way to each other; the best of friends and the worst of enemies, they hate each other with ease. They are envious, possess a poisonous tongue and a dry intellect, apt for learning differing things with ease; they are shrewd in all their doings'.

Andrea Camilleri: 'Sicilian friendship is a difficult art and perhaps one should call it by another name, fraternity, brotherhood, elective consanguinity. Something approaching a magic circle is created between two Sicilian friends which excludes all others, world affairs and even events from *history itself*.'

Leaving aside whether these generalisations have any truth to them or not, they certainly come equipped with a considerable literary weight. As with the chicken and the egg, we don't know if the myth forged the man or the man gave rise to the legend. Be that as it may, the people we have come across, the Sicilian of today, seems – at least on the surface – absolutely 'normal': Mediterranean Europeans of the twenty-first century.

A while ago I was talking to a friend about the Andalusians' struggle against their clichéd demons, surely very similar to the battle being fought by Sicilians. We find it pernicious that outside of our region we're seen as charming, idle, tireless party-goers. However, we easily give in to all these stereotypes, it takes a lot to resist acting like Andalusians. We could hate our image as eternal singers or dancers, although, at times, I think it has got under our very skin. We create – and *they create for us* – the cliché, and in turn the cliché moulds us, makes us in its image and likeness. Clearly, though, it's better to live with the image of happiness and wine than with the grim profile attributed to Sicilians. Let's just say that the cliché ends up being an inherited attribute of our personality. And as such, we're able to resign ourselves to it, even boast about it, or fight to correct or remove it from ourselves.

After taking for our breakfasts, the *signora* comes to the door to share out her goodbye kisses in just the emotional way my grandmother used to see us off, and to say goodbye in a straight forward Italian:

'*Buone vacanze a tutti!*'

THE KEYS MAKE CONTACT, the motor rumbles into action, Eureka is put to work once again. The next stop, almost a stone's throw away: Segesta, an ancient town surrounded by hills, where a small theatre and curious Greek temple still remain. 'Lands where the Greek is only found in the ruins laying on their sides in the thin grass, and not in the soul,' lamented Sciascia of his millennial Sicily, and perhaps without realising, using these words he summed up the sublime and tragic soul of Magna Grecia.

The temple at Segesta, unfinished, lacks a cella or roofed inner chamber and its columns are smooth, making it a very singular specimen. However, the most notable feature is the way in which it blends with the landscape, almost to the point where we pass it by. My beloved Zagajewski also agreed with this in a poem that explains the feeling very well:

Segesta
On the meadow a vast temple –
a wild animal
open to the sky.

FROM SEGESTA WE HEAD TOWARDS TRAPANI, a strip of urbanised land where, if we believe the historians, Charles V disembarked after his victory in Tunis. I've seen various drawings and tapestries reproducing this campaign in which the emperor subdued the fleet of Barbarossa, but none claiming to be his arrival in Sicily. This gives my imagination free rein to conjure visions where battalions of soldiers advance along these waysides, dragging amour and weapons, tired yet satisfied.

Halfway there, without any prior warning, Iván pulls over on to the hard shoulder. A road sign indicates that Trapani and Capaci are straight ahead; and off to the right, seaward bound, the Isole delle Femmine:

'The genuine *Isla Mujeres* as sung by our very own Javier Ruibal!' cries out Iván, who will be singing the chorus for the rest of the day, bewitched by the discovery: '*Tú la reina* *de Isla Mujeres / y yo, si tú me quieres, seré tu esclavo más fiel …'**

We scrutinise the horizon and, indeed, we do see the little island, glistening like a mountain of salt in the distance. We ask the girls to pose next to the sign, as an Isle of Women without women is a rather sad thing, and right there, with the song made *isola* as a distant witness, we promise to send the photo to Javier.

'I don't want to deflate you, but I think his song refers to Isla Mujeres in the Caribbean, where they held the African slave women who would be sold to the landowners,' points out Ro.

'I bet he has no idea this other one exists, he'll be just as delighted,' I add.

'Let's drop the subject,' says Iván. 'You're in full fetishistic pursuit of your Borges, I'll do the same with my Ruibal.'

In any case, our disembarkation in Trapani will be much less epic than that of Carolus V. A 'deceptively happy and unremarkable town', according to Durrell. I remember Italo Calvino being sure that there is no point in distinguishing between happy and unhappy cities, but rather between those that continue giving form to their desires through the centuries and those where the desires either manage to wipe out the city, or are wiped out by it.

Today the fog appears to have wiped out not only the desires, but the entire town. We enter blindfolded, and once we've crossed the belt of unpleasant modern buildings on the outskirts, we park near the sea – an infallible reference point – and decide upon a stroll around the centre. A provincial capital, but with the nature of a village in its hospitable appearance, and with a certain Andalusian air. Trapani is very walkable, in spite of the muggy overcast sky and humidity currently soaking the paving stones.

---

* 'You're the Queen of the Isle of Women / and I, if you love me, will be your most faithful slave …'

When the pedestrian lifts his gaze, the mixture so common to almost all Sicilian towns gives rise to an already familiar, but fascinating confusion: a baroque chapel followed by a simple seventies block of flats, next to which you find the hallway of a renaissance mansion, and then a rationalist office building, whilst further on there is a church with a nod to the gothic, the Catalan, or with a plateresque façade. Despite this historical stew, and aside from the fact it chimes with our personal taste, I think the city *works:* you notice an almost diplomatic respect amongst this baton change of cultures, a harmonic smoothness to the puzzle's final product.

Chance directs us to the food market, which is always a banquet for my senses, due to the fact that I spent long periods of my childhood playing in a Ceuta souk. I also link those happy moments with the smell of trodden fruit, of leftover ice impregnated with fish guts, and even with the flood from the hoses used to sweep the floor clean at the end of the day. Any market seems to me a circus of intense recollections, a marvellous and voluntary bewilderment. Trapani's proves to be no exception: as soon as I put foot inside it, my eyes and nostrils dilate to absorb everything surrounding me.

We buy olives, dried salted tuna – a long tradition in this town – and a little bread from an establishment christened with a sign displaying the singular name of 'Pane, Amore & Fantasia'.

'What more do we need to keep us happy,' I comment.

We skirt a frankly unkempt sea wall – urine and rubbish – leading out to a jetty, where gulls sit and then take flight. The site is both decadent and melancholic in equal measure. Does it put us in mind of somewhere?

'Cádiz,' says Ro. 'It's somewhat similar to the Campo del Sur.'

'Yes, but it's got a bit of Conil about it, don't you reckon?' adds Iván.

Leonardo Sciascia also found a similar kinship in his *Sicilian Uncles*: 'Cádiz was beautiful; it was like Trapani, but the whiteness of its houses was more luminous ...' Did Sciascia ever visit my town? The very idea fills me with enthusiasm, although I'm not especially fanatical about Cádiz, but Sciascia, yes.

Before leaving the town, we pass by the point known as the Lazzaretto, the leper colony. This was probably once an internment centre for the sick, which conjures up images of the oppressive atmosphere Bufalino recreated in his magnificent work *A Plague-spreader's Tale*.

The smell of the sea is intense and penetrating here, full of salt and the essence of seaweed. I lose my gaze to the distance with the vain illusion that I can make out the Egadi Islands, or, even more ambitiously, the Tunisian coast itself, towards which a cargo boat is now departing. Disappointingly, myopia only lets me reach an islet we could get to by walking or, in the worst-case scenario, by swimming and with little effort. I do feel like a dip, because the heat is starting to press down and the blue waters are calling me, but there's no time for that: we must get going.

A VERTIGINOUS MOUNTAIN ROAD takes us to Erice, from which we can contemplate Trapani and its entire peninsula. The city still seems to melt into the dense fog, to such an extent it has the illusion of being suspended in the air. As with the port of Messina, the spit of land supporting it takes the form of a very pronounced sickle or horn, an impression that becomes less obvious at ground level. I start to get a bit car sick with so many mountainous curves, but finally we arrive. We leave Eureka in a car park and breathe deeply the fresh, clear country air, strolling for a while among the practically empty streets.

When the ancient mariners used to arrive on the Sicilian coast, they say that the first thing the sailors spotted was this peak. By observing whether it was clear or obscured by cloud they would get a prediction of their voyage. Erice got its name from the son of Venus, and had an admirable temple dedicated to the Goddess of Fertility, upon which the Normans built the governor's palace. In the labyrinthine layout of the town you can find traces of the Arab presence, and in the walls surrounding it the old need to defend oneself, not only from the usual invaders, but also from an invisible enemy and one far more difficult to evade: the wind.

Today the air is fresh and gentle, preferable to the dog days we've been experiencing of late. We come to a church from the late Romanesque period, neighbour to a formidable tower that we enter for the modest price of one euro. Iván and Ka are the first to go straight up the tower via the narrow helicoidal staircase. From the top of the belfry we look over the terracotta town, the rows of little ridged roofs, the small toy-like houses as if belonging to a nativity scene. I read Fest: '… the town is constructed in porous sandstone and fragmented rock, all in the same pale grey colour, which gives it an archaic look, outside of any temporal concerns'. Seemingly, this timeless aspect is only external. Iván and Ka return disappointed by the church as its interior was restored in 1860, apparently with little style or taste.

'Fifty cents per person, at least they didn't require us to wear paper serviettes over our shoulders. Even the girl stinging us for the entrance fee had tattooed arms: more modern than the sinister ticket sellers in the capital,' they assure us.

We get comfortable in a nearby picnic spot and break open the bread and tins, whose flavour enthuses our friends to improvise a funny mock scene from the confessional:

'Father, I have to admit to eating dried salted tuna and tuna roe in the Trapani market.'

'Oh, my child, there is so much gullibility in the world! Don't you know that the tuna from Trapani comes from the devil?'

'I had no idea Father, I swear.'

'Free yourself from it immediately, or your palate and your throat will burn in the internal fires of hell, and only the holy water of Cavagrande, *non frizzante*, will be able to save you ...'

We take a digestive walk before saying goodbye to Erice, and I linger in front of a poster advertising the Ettore Majorana Cultural Centre. The building is closed, but thanks once more to Sciascia I know who has received this honour. Many will be surprised to know that Sicily hasn't only given the world writers, myths, tyrants and inquisitors: it was also the birthplace of a prodigious physicist, a scientist who disappeared without trace, giving rise to all manner of speculations. The most concrete among them is that he could have been the first to discover the coveted secret of the atomic bomb, and before claiming this dubious honour, passing into history as the pioneer of mass destruction, he preferred to abandon his calculations and take refuge in a closed monastery. It moves me to think of this learned man's refusal to be acclaimed as a new Doctor Moreau. When doing so, he would have already known that others would sooner or later arrive at the same findings. The world powers had set off a desperate race, sparing no resources in pursuit of the final goal, but they weren't open to cooperation. Majorana's great lesson, his last, wasn't of a scientific nature, but a moral one.

We can't leave this province without visiting the famous salt flats, the base of its economy since time immemorial. How do we get there? We ask some locals and they show us the way in the best and nicest manner possible: by getting into their car and simply saying, 'follow us'. We roll along for a while and then we're confronted by an expanse of estuaries, lagoons and windmills. Our guide-car turns around and, without further ado, waves goodbye. One can't ask for greater generosity.

For many the vast salt flat is an indisputably attractive and relaxing landscape. For me, thanks once again to Sciascia and his *Salt in the Wound*, it's also a testament to many generations of Sicilians who worked in very tough conditions. 'When the salt miners retire, with their pension of five thousand lire a month, they spend their days in the sun, which they believe will dry out all the humidity from their bones. But every night the bones begin to ache again.'

Much has been written about the island's economic dependence on two elemental fruits of the land and sea: salt and sulphur, not to mention their spiritual influence. Both abrasive, lethal, yet purifying, charged with symbolic powers, another metaphor for the close proximity maintained here between life and death. Maupassant, who got to visit the sulphur mines, was left shocked by the sight of children working at the pit face. 'They are ten or twelve years old, and they go up and down these steps fifteen times in a day, receiving a copper for each downward trip. They are small, thin, and yellow, with enormous and shining eyes ...' And at the same time as these emanations made them drop like flies, they also gave hundreds of families a living.

The same could be said of the salt flats, scattered with picturesque windmills that today simply act as a decorative element. 'Wherever one looks, salt in Sicily has become a force, a condition and a destiny,' said Gesualdo Bufalino. In front of these glittering mountains, impeccably formed squadrons, one can't help but give in to an odd feeling of distaste, a sense of impotence, and if it weren't for so much salt, I could only classify it as bitterness.

MARSALA IS A TOWN you could easily bypass on any whistle-stop tour around the island. However, Ro has to check some exam grades on email, so we head for the centre in search of a cibercafé. I watch the animated toing and froing of the locals in the streets as I try a glass of the full-bodied wine named after the locality, similar to sweet oloroso, which sharp English wine merchants brought to world fame. I also study an evocative print of Garibaldi's landing on this soil in 1860, with all his soldiers – the famous thousand – their horses and those women who seem like escapees from the palette of

Cruz Herrera. Much more colourful, surely, than the other landing, not so far off in time, of the US marines on this very same beach. Such an association of ideas even leads me to find a certain similarity between Marsala and Rota. But a Phoenician like me has no choice other than to feel at home in what was a vital enclave of the kingdom, however much the modern day town is a distant echo of lost splendours.

AN HOUR LATER we're in Marinella, another hard to find little coastal village, a stone's throw from Selinunte, on whose beach we'll spend the night. Whatever exertions we go through, Sicily keeps on compensating us with the most beautiful sights: the summer spreads its hot and penetrating scents, the streets are peaceful, the water tranquil as a lake. Marinella is idyllic and we won't be the ones to break the spell. Borges had already glimpsed this, the fact that beauty, like happiness, is commonplace, and that not one day passes without it unfurling before us. We only have to open our eyes to see it.

I gaze at the delicious, whiter than white, pregnant moon, silver-plating the sea. We eat our sandwiches out on the jetty where the placid locals are casting their fishing rods. Afterwards we stretch out our sleeping bags in the middle of a rock circle over warm, soft sand on the ultimate paradise beach.

Marinella, Selinunte

I T'S ABOUT AN HOUR until dawn. If I were Pepe Caballero Bonald, I would surely write that I thought I'd seen it, but I don't know if I did, maybe I was certain, but perhaps there was a distortion of the senses, conjuring up a false perception of reality, allowing me to wander in the unfathomable labyrinths of memory, one of those phantasmagorical dreamlike experiences provoked by who knows what stimulus of the subconscious ... Well, this is leading to one of those interminable circles, which inevitably end in readers' protests: take note, yes you did see it, so much the better, write about it. And if not, enough of the blahblahblah, invent it, you're not a writer for nothing.

I saw it. First came the barking that woke us. Then a splashing noise growing closer in the tranquil waters, still well lit by the dying rays of the moon. And finally the canine figure, silhouetted against the light, panting a couple of metres away from our camp. A black dog like a bad omen, with a distinctly unfriendly air, motionless before us, seemingly a devil from the sea, with teeth already bared, ferocious and yellowy, eyes glistening like silver dollars, as they would say in the novels of Marcial Lafuente Estefanía.*

Terrified, Ro hugs me. I ask her to keep calm, and above all

---

* José Manuel Caballero Bonald is a poet and writer born in Jerez, known for his careful use of language and baroque style. Marcial Lafuente Estefanía was a Spanish writer of Westerns.

not to make any sudden movements. After studying us carefully, the animal walks away. We then see the boats hung with lanterns, the sailors shouting to other dogs. We hear them wandering around all over the beach, rubbing their paws amongst the rocks. Although scared to death of an attack from a pack of hell hounds, the image is a beautiful one.

We recover from the fright whilst dawn breaks. The other two have already roused themselves and are starting to clear up the camp. Eureka appears to have slept well and looks ready for a new day. With the memory of the diabolical dog losing force, I delight in contemplating the sea, which has taken on an especially beautiful colour as the sun rises. For an inhabitant of Cádiz, except for the odd, harsh – yet now faded – episode of its history, the sea is a bringer of glad tidings, a fount of riches, symbol of light, grace and happiness. However, I've read that Sicilians have always wanted to live facing away from the sea, looking towards the interior and thus denying the fact they live on an island, an island where the briny waves in sayings and popular songs bring indescribable fears. 'The sea is bitter', says a popular proverb. 'Sing to the sea, but cling to the ropes', insists another. 'Whoever can go by land never goes by sea.' The maritime route has seen the arrival of Berbers, Normans, Lombards, Catalans, the armies of Charles V and Louis XIV, Piedmontese, Austrians, the supporters of Garibaldi, Algerian pirates, and even the troops of Patton and Montgomery. None sounded the pipes of peace, but the drums of discord and pillage. And when it wasn't a question of weaponry, it was disease or the no less lethal imposition of taxes. These all-conquering assaults must have inspired the children's story by Dino Buzzati, *The Bears' Famous Invasion of Sicily*, which was very well illustrated by the author himself. Without doubt these storybook plantigrades were the nicest invaders Sicily has ever had.

THE EARLY START means we get to the ruins at Selinunte before they have opened the ticket office. We're ready to visit one of the most important archaeological centres in the entire Mediterranean, the Hellenists' Disneyland. We kill time by looking at the enormous model displayed inside a glass box at the entrance, but it hardly gives us an idea of the formidable dimensions of the place. When we finally get our four entrance tickets, we notice a curious detail. All the *biglietti* sold which allow access to the island's historic/artistic monuments have the same image, but this time it coincides with the object of our visit: the Acropolis of Selinunte.

As soon as we enter, we see a vast expanse of grassland, isolated from everywhere else by some artificial hills. In front is the sea, a dark blue sea, 'a wine-dark sea' spattered with glimmers of light as the sun rises in the sky.

'Your first impression is one of great loneliness and melancholy,' I read in the book *Sicilian Carousel*. It has been said that many travellers came here in search of the poetic breath of the past and all they stumbled across was plain and simple archaeology. Perhaps a vision of decadence runs through the Romantic spirit creating depressing associations of ideas, but for us, this morning, the place is a miracle of light and sea breezes. For such scenery, our forebears were in a class of their own. 'What landscape-tasters the ancient Greeks were!' – we agree with Durrell, they knew what they were doing when they planted their flag here.

Taking a few strides to the right, we reach temples E, F and G. They weren't initially dedicated to letters of the alphabet, however: it's fair to guess that archaeologists didn't know in honour of which gods the temples were consecrated, so gave them these names which remain today. Borges also enjoyed this fact. Scianna remembers the following: 'He is fascinated when we tell him that the temples, to whom they are dedicated we know not, are assigned letters of the alphabet. Nothing seems more apt to him than this deification of the alphabet. "Temple C for Conrad, for example. Isn't it fitting to dedicate a temple to Conrad?" They suggest to him a temple dedicated to Borges. "Better to Buster Keaton".

The best of them, or at least the better restored, is without doubt E. We skirt around it, passing its Doric columns and walking along its rectangular floor with an intense feeling of wellbeing. Nevertheless, Iván is suspicious of the reconstruction:

'I thought that when the experts arrived, around 1960, there wasn't a single stone still left standing. I bet they used a few shovelfuls of concrete.'

Temple F, although totally levelled, let's say wholeheartedly ruined, is much more striking. The columns are so enormous that, we reckon, they couldn't find cranes sufficiently sturdy enough to put them back on their feet. The people from Segesta, who no doubt envied the beauty of Selinunte, according to legend allied themselves to Carthage, and a siege ensued which destroyed this settlement and sparked off a massacre. Without doubt, fearsome earthquakes would have also swept across the area. With the great numbers killed in barely two hundred years, Selinunte, itself, fell into disrepair.

I see the girls photographing each other among the ruins, insignificant little figures between the huge toppled pieces. They remind me of a photograph of Asplund in the Paestum Acropolis, where he looks like Gulliver in the land of the giants. The traveller generally likes disproportionate sizes, it's one of the favourite things to talk about back at home: pyramids, temples, obelisks, beautiful or otherwise, but above all *big*. They transmit a sensation of amazing strength, and as if strength isn't enough, their intelligent conception is astonishing.

I've also found some impressions jotted down by Albert Speer, Hitler's chief architect, during his visit to Sicily in March 1939: 'When contemplating the temples of Selinunte and Agrigento I was able to confirm, with deep satisfaction, that even the Ancients hadn't escaped from megalomania. It

Selinunte, 1984

was evident how, here, the colonial Greeks put to one side the principle of moderation they so praised in their home-land.' Subsequently, Nazi architecture – of which I've seen the occasional trace, for example, along the quay in Messina – wanted to emulate this feeling of magnificence. Frankly, apart from the horror of National Socialism as a political system, I think they often built well.

Some tourists slowly begin to arrive. We're left to our own devices, clambering over the millennial remains; the others search out good views for their cameras, while I go hunting for the first photo of Borges at the Acropolis. The maestro is seated on a structure appearing to be a stone quadrilateral, seemingly a house that has lost its walls, which was then devoured by nature, but not sufficiently enough to obscure the form of the original floor plan. I look around and see nothing fitting the bill.

'The sea is in the background. It has to be over there,' says Ro, pointing into the distance, where we see another shape-less pile of stones and some upright columns.

We walk in that direction, crossing a rugged patch of brambles and shrubs. Iván stops to pick berries, and without the least fear of poisoning himself starts to chew them in an unhurried fashion. The truth is I can't imagine Borges and María Kodama up to their waists in this miniature forest. 'Good heavens, María, they have a fragrance that reminds one of the taste of lychees!' Scianna reports the maestro saying. Then I see a little train transporting tourists from one part of the necropolis to another, as well as some mini-carts, like those used on golf courses.

In any case, Borges was tired when he arrived at this point, where the ruins of the six temples are spread out. The expres-sion on his face, the way in which his body is resting and his hands lay on the cane indicate he was in need of a break. I immediately look to the unmistakable pattern of the stones, and use their form and the configuration of the crevices as a guide to find the exact point where the Argentinean placed his eminent bottom. There's no doubt, even the telegraph poles are still in place. Borges appears with his hair a little tousled, perhaps owing to a breeze similar to the one blowing this morning, or to the fact that he passed a hand through his hair, unintentionally ruffling it. The sea seeming so wide in the photograph is partly due to the tilt of the land, but also to the skill of the photographer, who has managed to get a very attractive result.

Scianna asks himself what Borges has come to find in Sicily. The Argentinean provides an answer: 'This island has an extraordinary importance for me. Here, in front of these stones, this sea, which is the same and yet not the same, man was to abandon the realm of simple emotion, in order to start constructing a system of enquiry.'

I peer out towards the sea, beyond the Borgesian 'wire fences that are an affront to the countryside ...' I've heard that this place wasn't as well guarded in the past as now, so backpackers could spend the night under the stars in such a tremendous setting. If it wasn't for the little time we have left, I'd suggest that we run the risk and camp here.

I have a feeling that I'm on the same stone as Borges. It's quite hot, the birds are singing, the waves are sighing below, licking the sand of a deserted beach, one which invites you to take a swim. I turn back to look straight ahead, where Iván is pointedly looking at me, as if expecting me to break into Anglo-Saxon poetry at any moment.

'Well, what do you see?' he asks me.

'If you move to one side, the next photograph in the series.'

This time it must have been coincidence, or don't we agree about the non-existence of coincidences? Certainly, though, I've studied the little red book enough to remember the image all of a sudden and identify the setting immediately.

Borges is turned away from the camera, his straight grey hairs hiding the venerable tonsure. In front of him

Selinunte, 1984

archaeological remains are piled up in a random manner. And in the background the row of upright columns still support what's left of the capital. Scianna probably just positioned himself behind the maestro's back to take the shot, without any need to bother him, leaving him to sit quietly on his stone. The photographer must have truly had to make an effort with the focus, as my compact camera is hardly able to fit in the whole ensemble. But regards the positioning I've got no doubts: the broken column standing out in the centre of the image, showing a diagonal crack, is still there almost twenty years later, with exactly the same tilt.

Setting aside my Borgesian passion, the shot looks very attractive, very poetic: the aged man, who perhaps feels the proximity of death, scrutinises the remains of a distant civilisation. The ruined architecture still whispers the splendour of its people. Only one thing is missing, hardly any trace of what life would have been like here in this now devastated scene so attractively located by the waters of the Mediterranean, where a pair of rigid eyes wanted to gaze upon decline itself, as if into a mirror.

Scianna recounts his tale once more. The maestro is tired, but hasn't lost his sense of humour: 'What a surprise for these ruins, to be visited by another old ruin!'

I then recall some words Borges dedicated to the Greek Temple of Poseidon:

> There is nothing in the world that is not mysterious,
> but the mystery is more evident
> in certain things than in others:
> in the sea, in the eyes of the elders,
> in the colour yellow and in music.

I turn once more towards the beach, towards the invincible sea, already completely dazzled by the powerful southern sun. I'm stuck like this, spellbound, for who knows how long. Until Iván puts a hand on my shoulder and says:

'What's with the daft smile? Come on, we ought to think about going.'

'Don't even think about it,' I say to him rather sharply. 'There's one photograph in the series left to find.'

I show the others this magnificent portrait of Borges, gently picked out against the light, with the twisted branches of a tree behind him, webbing the sky – another somewhat metaphorical composition, as if his head were the spot germinating these fantastical branching ramifications. Our poor knowledge of botany doesn't stretch to identifying the species of tree. We're also unaware of the type of trees or bushes creeping into the lower part of the photograph. I'm sure the picture has been used as the cover for some other book, although I can't recall which one.

'Are you mad,' says Ka emphatically. 'Scianna took this two decades ago. The chances of the tree not being cut down or dead are so small.'

'Perhaps the photo was taken in autumn, once the leaves had fallen. If so, it would now be doubly unrecognisable,' points out Ro. However, my blindness is more stubborn than that of Borges, Homer and Milton put together, thus I find myself exploring the whole place, from the Acropolis to what remains of the Temple of Malophoros, and from there once again over temples E, F and G, without any success. I'm like a child enraged by a whim impossible to satisfy, or a very dim-witted thief who has forgotten where he hid the loot.

Finally I come across a specimen that reminds me of the image. It's a little tree with skeletal branches, burnt by the sun. The knots appearing on Borges' tree are nowhere to be seen. Besides, a type of hut exists in the background that is totally absent from Scianna's photo.

'Listen, even in your wildest dreams that isn't the tree you're looking for. It's nothing like it!' protests Iván.

Nevertheless, when he sees that I'm happy with the

Selinunte, 1984

substitute, he gives me an understanding pat on the back and
starts to walk towards the exit.

❧

THE LITTLE RED BOOK SAYS WE SHOULD HEAD for
Palermo, but it would be a step in the wrong direction: we
know that the famous Adonis in question was transferred
from the capital to the nearby town of Castelvetrano. It's in
this direction we must point Eureka.

Crossing a landscape of sown fields, we reach the place
in question, another terracotta settlement, criss-crossed by
alleyways and bleached, as we feared, by a suffocating heat.
In Greek times, it was akin to the warehouse for the populace
of Selinunte. Frederick II gave the gubernatorial reins to the
Tagliavia family, for them to pass into the hands of the Pig-
natelli Aragonas, who provided the town with some worthy
monuments. As with any good Sicilian town, there is a central
square, which, like so many others, takes the name Garibaldi.
Very close by is the entrance to the Museo Civico: as far as we
know, the only one in Castelvetrano and the surrounding area.

Scianna's photograph shows an out of focus sculptural

Palermo, 1984: Before the Adonis

silhouette very much to the fore, with the figure of Borges supposedly passing by whilst paying the statue little attention. Yet if we merge the distances involved, he also allows himself to be touched by the hands of the Adonis.

As the Museo Civico is a mini-museum, practically one room, we immediately find the desired object. In fact, it's the jewel of the collection, and very esteemed judging by the locals, who have christened it with the nickname *Il Pupo*, or 'the puppet'. It's a Greek bronze, originally from Selinunte, made in 460 BC. Any objections Iván? The eyes seem disproportionately large, but the form is slender, delicate, one could say finished with love, although the girls reckon the bottom is larger than the ideal would suggest. I test out my senses with very poor results: the room smells of nothing, we can't touch anything, if we're silent the only audible sound is the hum of the air conditioning.

Things have changed since the image of Borges was taken; they've now protected the sculpture with a glass case, thereby making it impossible to take a photo under the same conditions. It's also hemmed in by display cabinets full of other, less historically valuable objects: Roman lamps, Greek ceramics, Punic amphorae, worn out coins of diverse origin and age. Among them, the girls are greatly amused to find a collection of erotic artefacts worked in stone, or at least that's their Freudian interpretation.

But we've no time for archaeological obscenities; mission accomplished, let's get on with the safari.

Eraclea Minoa, Agrigento, San Leone

I'VE BEEN SLEEPING for quite a while, half-opening my eyes to stare at the landmarks so I don't miss the undulating parched countryside on both sides of the road, the 'deserted fertility' Goethe saw in Sicily's wheat fields.

It must be said, the heat is suffocating and could cause hallucinations if it weren't for the fact that I'm worn out, exhausted. We stop at the famous Eraclea Minoa beach, named after Minos, king of Crete, who pursued Dedalus here. But, yet again, the landscape doesn't so much resemble the clarion call of mythology as the ideal of bucolic Greece, the simple light that bathed Virgil.

The shoreline extends towards a pine forest, and the water seems reasonably clear. It's a shame jellyfish are once again visible through the transparent surface. Now we understand why the Gorgon is the symbol of Sicily, although they say the solution to all ills lies in her gaze.

'I've got more faith in ammonia,' mutters Ka, and she wipes her salve stick across the still livid scar from the sting.

If the jellyfish weren't enough, wasps fly over us in crowded, threatening swarms between the trees. We have an uncomfortable rather than pleasant lunch, sunbathe for a while and get back on the road, heading for Agrigento.

A wind
that stains and gnaws the sandstone and the heart

of the doleful telamons lying
felled on the grass ...

So said Quasimodo of this route leading us to what was once Girgenti, the former Greek homeland of Empedocles, Carthaginian, then Roman, Byzantine, and now, judging by what we can see from the road, huge, out of proportion and polluted.

In an outer lying car park, the Mediterranean's most slovenly gorilla – curly pony tail, cut-off t-shirt and exposed belly, swimming trunks in a patriotic stars and stripes design, hiking boats and socks – bleeds two euros from us to look after Eureka. And we have to pay another two each to gain entrance to the nearby Valley of the Temples.

'These ruins are going to be our ruin,' sighs Ka.

The magnificent collection making up the Valley of the Temples is a counterpoint to Selinunte's Acropolis, which seemed to sit so well in the landscape it was difficult to distinguish the work of man from that of nature. In Agrigento, on the contrary, the Greek constructions look like they're being pursued by the modern city. It's as if an army of tenement blocks from the fifties were about to fall upon the ancient stones at any moment, thereby devouring them. Five Doric temples, hexastyle in origin, confront this despicable curtain with the red dusky tones of their calcareous stone. As we walk among them, the aggressive external interferences – from the urban smog to the traffic noise – make it very difficult to imagine how this place would have been, not just in the time of Virgil, but even when it left Maupassant open mouthed.

In any event, the proportions are more graceful and easier to grasp, less superhuman than Selinunte appeared to be. But Iván still has no confidence in the wonderful set design created by the grouping:

'This temple was preserved because it was a Christian basilica ...' he says a little peeved. 'Another was restored by the

Romans ... two were rebuilt in the twentieth century ... and as for the Temple of Zeus, which theoretically had columns of almost 20 metres, not one stone looks remotely intact ...'

'I guess what they're giving us here is an approximate reconstruction,' I offer. 'What I don't get is why they don't just explain this honestly to the public. As if it wasn't enough of an effort to remake all this fallen antiquity, the archaeologists seem to be afraid visitors will feel cheated if they discover that a column wasn't exactly in this spot, but really over there.'

'The only truly Greek thing here are my sandals ... and I bought them in Morocco!'

Perhaps Iván would be pleased to know that in one of his stories Lampedusa goes much further; sharpening his proverbial ironic wit, he assures us that all the Greek temples on the island are second hand and, to crown it all, 'very recent'.

What remains unquestionable is the powerful scenographic effect of the valley. Not of the temples as individual structures, but of the collection as a whole. When you half-close your eyes, for a moment you could be in front of one of those gigantic opera sets, painted by hand in minute detail, the kind they rarely make these days. Whether real or imaginary, both invariably recreate the past in an amazing way, they stir up true emotions however little we contribute. 'They make the imagination travel, they strike the senses like a blow between the eyes,' Voillet-le-Duc would enthusiastically say in a letter to his father. 'I understood ancient architecture by being there, as I understood poetry by reading Homer.'

In order to placate Iván's peevishness, I put an end to the string of quotes by finally giving him another salvo of verses by Quasimodo, dedicated to the Temple of Zeus:

In silence we regard this hint
of ironic falsehood: for us the diurnal
moon burns upside down and falls
in the vertical fire. What future is there
to read in the Doric well, what past?

'OK, I surrender,' my friend accepts. 'Let's go back to Eureka, and the twenty-first century.'

Our spectators' gaze is also definitely tired of ruins. It's bored of being amazed. We've spent a week rushing around at full tilt, snapping away, almost without time to process the information. We reckon that a leisurely stroll around Sicily's principal attractions would need at least two or three months. By now, at the pace we've been maintaining, our capacity for amazement has almost been squeezed dry.

AGRIGENTO, THE MOST SPLENDID CITY in the world according to Pindar, but also the most perishable. For Brancati, narrow, cramped, tortuously closed-in on itself. In the words of Sciascia, 'so twisted and disorganised that it looks like one of those shapes made by a baby's arms and legs in the crib. All the squares are on such an incline they seem to be on the point of sliding on top of each other ...' This isn't at all misleading: Agrigento does have a bit of the Piranesian labyrinth about it, with a touch of Russian doll, or better still, of the anarchic inward-looking aura of the *kasbah*. There are cities with the outline of a circulatory system, and others like Agrigento that have more of a digestive one. At least that's how it appears this afternoon.

We walk absent-mindedly through the modern city, through the Montelusa and Vigàta of the writer Camilleri and his detective Montalbano. There is something in the novels of Camilleri, in addition to the delicious recipe book of Sicilian gastronomy, something I now notice in the atmosphere of these streets, in the gestures and way of speaking used by the people – it's the tremendously real mixture of tragedy and comic opera. Some passers-by, like the fictional characters, seem caricatures of themselves, as if they've sprung from those absurdly eroto-comic films starring the prankster Alvaro Vitali. Yet at the same time, Camilleri's plot lines, from the tales of rough-and-ready murderers to the very modern illegal trafficking of immigrants, are truly tough backdrops, little suited to humour. Here in Agrigento, I feel the writer, and perhaps, indeed, the city, is determined to superimpose a false smile on the face of pain: somewhat similar to painting moustaches on death itself.

The steep slopes are next to catch my attention; bordered by steps, they veer off from the main streets and – according once more to Sciascia – 'abandon the traveller in the most beautiful part of town, sorry for having made him climb upwards'; an attractive personification! I'd like to see the water run through here on a rainy day.

At the end of one of these, chosen by chance, we come across an open-air *trattoria* where we sit down to the cheapest meal of our trip, and also the most pleasant. Three very tasty gigantic pizzas, various glasses of marsala, soft drinks and the music of Miles Davies on the loudspeakers, all for the justified price of twenty-eight euros. It's a shame we can't remember the name of the establishment, nor does it figure on the bill, although we keep it in case someone doesn't believe us.

Eureka dodges mopeds, groups of friends heading for the clubs, teenagers knocking back alcopops, and the occasional traffic jam, in order to get to San Leone, Agrigento's beach. We intend to spend the night at the Internazionale campsite, which appears to be open but without anyone on the gate. Everything is deserted. After we do the rounds a couple of times, almost in the dark, we find the bar – a place with a rush mat roof near the beach – and two guys who look rather the worst for wear. One of them assures us he's the boss and rents us some scruffy bungalows with camp beds, at a very low price.

Sat facing the sea, we look back on the fun we've had on this journey while Iván opens a bottle of grappa he bought to toast our days here. He reads the label as if he's about to try some medicine: '*Julia Nova, dal gusto morbido, di transparenza cristallina e fraganza floreale*.* Forty degrees added to the thirty-five in temperature we must be experiencing this evening, fire on fire. We propose the toast:

'Here's to the four of us meeting up again for another trip.'

I already know that it'll never happen, we'll never all go on holiday together again, but it's the intention that counts. We clink our plastic cups without any noticeable sound, and raise them to our lips.

The grappa seems undrinkable. Ro tries to mix it with ice and coke, but the result is dreadful. Ka and I empty our glasses discreetly on to the sand. I remember Lawrence Durrell was also given a swig of this atrocious potion: '... like drinking fumed oak in liquid form. Heartening stuff,' was his reaction.

Only Iván joyously treats himself to large gulps, which will later make him wander around the campsite like a ghost obviously confusing the door to his room.

⁓

I love this photograph. Borges is talking to a Palermitan musician, Severino Gazzelloni, a flautist judging by the image. I doubt that professionals like him take their instrument of work everywhere, so without any basis, it makes sense to assume the meeting took place after a recital: Gazzelloni has played for the maestro, probably at a public performance. Afterwards, Borges goes to congratulate him. His expression is serious, one of respect and curiosity, facing the admiring, friendly smile of Gazzelloni.

As a first impression, the Argentinean seems to be receiving the flute as a gift. After all, famous authors are honoured with all kinds of presents wherever they go. But I don't think this is the case, a good musician never gets rid of his instrument. In any event, he's giving the gift of music, but not its source, the beloved object with which he earns a crust. He's only showing it to him.

---

* 'Julia Nova, crystal clear, with a delicate taste and floral notes'.

Palermo, 1984: With the musician Severino Gazzelloni

I have taken it for granted that Gazzelloni is a good musician, but have to prove it with my own ears. Is he a classical player, a jazzman? Perhaps he practices some traditional Sicilian form? Does he play as a soloist, or form part of some orchestra? In order to satisfy my curiosity, I look everywhere for a record of his. However, they're not so easy to find.

'*Gazzellone?*' I was asked by a perplexed record seller in Palermo.

In the end I found an album of his on a stall in Agrigento. *Il flauto d'oro* is how they present him commercially.* *Emozioni in pop* is the name of the record, with *elaborazione per il flauto Gianni Ferrio*. I must admit the repertoire isn't exactly groundbreaking. There's a none too elaborate version of *Aguas de marzo* by Jobim, an *Upa negrito* by Gianfrancesco Guarnieri and Edu Lobo with arrangements of wind instruments, a song by Mina, and other pieces I don't know but which sound too simple in their execution, rather like piped music, if that's not too cheeky. The flautist plays with

---

* Gazzelloni is marketed as the 'Golden Flute'.

a certain natural grace, but there are no displays of virtuosity or any edge to his work. It's a smooth and indulgent sound. Perhaps Borges, who wasn't renowned for his musical taste, wouldn't have found these renditions unpleasant. However, it's also possible they may have unleashed his most pitiless criticism, reserved for almost everything that wasn't Brahms, thus marking them out as tedious.

AFTER HIS VISIT TO SICILY, the maestro referred to the island's music during an interview. 'I was surprised when I heard the local music, I heard an individual playing the guitar, a man from the country, they told me he was playing local folk tracks, and they sounded like those Creole tunes from Buenos Aires province or from Uruguay: those tunes set to the poetry of *La tapera*, or *El gaucho* by Elías Regules. Well, that's exactly the type of music I heard in Sicily.' The truth is I don't overly trust the maestro's musical inclinations. Anyway, I'm sure he enjoyed Gazzelloni's conversation more than his music, a language he was never able to master, an ability never passed down to him from on high.

Although I consider myself to be a fervent lover of music, I realise I hardly know anything of Sicilian music. I'm aware of the Catanese Franco Battiato and his lyrical, danceable yet introspective songs, as he was enormously popular in Spain for a while, until the whims of fashion changed. I also have a record at home called *Canto di Malavita*, advertised as *la música de la mafia*: a series of Calabrian songs with a particular provincial atmosphere, too imbued with local colour for me to pretend that I understand more than a certain uneasiness, their air of violence on the paved streets. They transmit an earthy, ancestral whisper, like the cries of flamenco, but very far from the unrestrained, heart-rending nature of our *cante jondo*.*

---

* *Cante jondo*, or 'deep song', is a very traditional vocal style, said by many to be the heart and soul of Andalusian flamenco.

In a novel by Consolo, the enjoyable and lewd lyrics from *La Tubbiana* were reproduced, one of the island's typical carnival songs, whose words had seemingly been lost since the beginning of the twentieth century.

I recall the parties in Coppola's *The Godfather*, where the entire family sing along to lyrics of a childish rudeness set to very basic melodies. Moreover, in the third instalment of the saga, the tremendous *Cavalleria Rusticana* is performed, the well-known opera set in Sicily, even though its composer, Pietro Mascagni, was a native of Livorno in Tuscany. The work, based on a novel by Giovanni Verga, deals with a blood feud amongst peasants. *Bel canto* with knives would be a good explanation.

I've also seen the brilliant Sicilian trumpeter, Roy Paci, play live, and he's more than capable of kicking up a storm in his performances, although the ska rhythms and his melodies owe more to the cosmopolitan sounds of Mano Negra and the enthusiastic party-goer than to any regional tradition.

Maupassant, on his travels, attended a concert in Palermo, but was surprised by the musical passions of the Sicilians. In his travelogue he tells us *Carmen* was in fashion at the time, and that respectable citizens participated in the concert with a great deal of fervour. '... loving music to distraction, the entire crowd becomes a sort of vibrating beast that feels but doesn't reason. In five minutes, the same performer is applauded with enthusiasm and whistled with frenzy; the crowd stamps with joy or anger, and if some false note escapes from the singer's throat, a strange cry, exasperated, over shrill issues from all mouths at the same time.' I wonder if any such love for music has remained on the island that established *omertà*, the law of silence.

It would be a shame if nobody made the effort to save the musical memory of the people here. As a wise man once said, the task of reconstruction should not only be for the eyes, but also the ears. In the end, one gets the perhaps misguided impression that Sicily isn't a very musical place. Significantly,

Sciascia pointed out the fact that the island has never had a choral tradition. As music is also communication, it's an understanding of the other, as well as an ordered harmonic system, even in its most anarchic manifestations like free jazz. It makes me sad to think, if this land has been deaf and dumb to music, how the soul of its people may have been filled instead by a cacophony from inside.

However, the photograph from the little red book still moves me. I like the gesture made by Gazzelloni as he lets Borges stroke the metal and try out the keys. A blind man who carries on hearing music through touch, perhaps caressing the flute to try and feel the soul of the instrument, to picture how the mechanism, with the help of pulsating human breath, will give rise to the blessed miracle of music.

Racalmuto, Enna, Messina

THE LAST DAY of our Sicilian journey. We all wake up with chronic backache and clear our heads by drinking coffee with a slightly salty taste before deciding between three options:

i) To visit the town of Corleone, the very one that inspired Puzo's novel *The Godfather*. Ruled out as soon as we imagine cafés with photos of Marlon Brando or shops called *La famiglia* selling souvenirs. It's not so unlikely: Ro tells us how she saw a dental clinic in Fuente Vaqueros with the name Lorcadent.

ii) To search the map for Pirandello's birthplace, a spot poetically called Caos. According to the tourist information, his house is now a museum and the grounds have a hundred-year-old pine tree under which the writer used to look for inspiration. After the episode of the Borgesian tree in Selinunte, the others don't want to know about this idea. Ruled out.

iii) To take the route to Racalmuto, hometown of Leonardo Sciascia. This option wins in the end: we think a journey around Borgesian Sicily wouldn't be complete without a visit to the birthplace of one of his greatest admirers.

I valued Sciascia even before I'd read a word of his work. It's not the only time a writer has convinced me by just seeing his photo. It's enough to study any portrait of Leonardo Sciascia to glimpse in his eyes, in his hands – one in his pocket, the other always holding a cigarette – in his posture when walking, in the straightness of his back, many of the attributes of his work: truth, honesty, love of life, rigor and humanity. I've never been wrong about this. When I think of Blas de Otero and Borges himself, with such people first impressions are rarely misleading. They are, in themselves, open books, and this transparency reveals their lucidity, their heart and their genius.

In the ten years I spent studying Law, without any vocation, benefit or motivation, I can honestly say that I learnt more about justice reading Sciascia than from burying myself in any manual or book of statutes. If one takes the abstract concept of a set of scales, he aspires to tip the balance towards a positive future, towards bearing the best fruit possible from the human condition, the natural tendency for any decent society.

I also think the man from Racalmuto had all the requisites to be worthy of a Nobel Prize: his work is sufficiently vast, coherent, and truly involved with the world in which he lived. Why did he never get one? Maybe it was due to his premature death. Or perhaps because three Sicilian Nobel laureates in one century – Quasimodo and Pirandello came before – were judged by the Swedish Academy as too many for such a small island. He also shares this fate with Borges, although I doubt Sciascia would have lost sleep over the prospect of such glittering prizes. I'm convinced his most longed-for reward was the holiday time he spent writing at his house in Noce, in his beloved hometown, rereading Stendhal, enjoying his grandchildren.

A short while ago I was asked the classic question about which books I'd take to a desert island, and I was tempted to answer that it would have to be the complete works of Sciascia. I immediately changed my mind as it occurred to me that reading Sciascia makes no sense on a desert island; his books require you to lift your gaze after every paragraph and confront what you've just read by looking at what is happening around you, at all of humanity's heroic deeds and miseries.

Sciascia's world doesn't replace life, or seek to avoid it, but penetrates and decodes it, charged as his work is with all life's horror and wonder.

Be that as it may, a figure like him doesn't deserve to be born in such a sad place as Racalmuto, so untouched by the hand of God. At least those are our thoughts when we see the horrendous sports centre on the outskirts and enter the rather dirty streets redolent with such a lifeless atmosphere. Even the etymology backs up this impression: Racalmuto comes from the Arabic *Rahal-maut*, which means 'town of the dead', African conquerors having found it desolate due to an outbreak of plague. However, thinking about it, maybe a spirit like the great man's could only be forged in a depressed place such as this, where it's easy to imagine how it would have been forty or fifty years ago, with its poverty multiplied and with all the millennial weight of its history, the inherited memory whose force Sciascia explained by turning to an idea of Borges': 'I believe my birth is subsequent to my residence here. I was already residing here, and then I was born.'

A loaded mule passes by us, spurred on by the slaps of its owner. The motorised vehicles all appear to be covered by a few centimetres of earthy dust, as if they've been parked up for quite some time. We take a couple of turns round the streets under the surprised yet watchful eye of the few pedestrians, until we reach the Sciascia foundation, located in what was the Convent of Santa Clara.

The building seems to have been recently renovated and everything smells new. So much so we can't find as many fetishistic traces of Don Leonardo as I would have wished. On the ground floor they have opened an exhibition showing marvellous images of Sicily, Mexico and India by Ferdinando Scianna. If it wasn't for the information plaques, in many cases it would be difficult to work out which image belonged to which location.

On one of the other floors, after a payment of another two euros each, we gain entry to an exhibition of rare editions and translations of Sciascia's work, protected by thick glass, as well as his collection of drawings hung around the walls. It's not that the author of *One Way or Another* was an artist: it seems he collected portraits and caricatures of writers he admired. A little sign points this out to us:

'*Ignoto a me stesso. Ritratti di scrittori da E. A. Poe a Jorge Luis Borges.*'

Among the pieces on display there is even a modest Chagall original. Of those represented I recognise a few illustrious French writers, whom I know fascinated him: Voltaire, Rousseau, Diderot ... Finally, between a Byron and a Rotterdam, I make out two pencil portraits of Borges, one as a young man and another much older, signed by a Gaetano Tranchino, the Siracusan surrealist painter.

With some of my remaining euros I buy a book of photographs showing Sciascia and Gesualdo Bufalino, friends but very different from one another. The man from Racalmuto was always involved in society's problems, maintaining his faith in the power of words, if not to change the world, at least to shake from complacency those ready to look beyond the end of their own noses. Bufalino, despaired of by his medics, spent his life absorbed in a private and intimate dialogue with literature, crafting precious sentences like a goldsmith, but unnoticed by the market and its readers, at least that's what he had us believe.

Albeit from different vantages, I feel the work of both writers gets to the essence of mankind; both achieve a purity in their literature because they are pure life translated into language; their characters pulsate, feel and suffer with us. And although the same can be said of many other contemporary authors, in few cases would it be so true as with these two Sicilians.

Such intense signs of wisdom and kindness on both faces. Sciascia is serious, Bufalino more relaxed, with his dark glasses hiding his wandering pupils. In various photos I finally discover our own comrade Ferdinando Scianna: very short, with scant hair and a trimmed grey beard. Vincenzo Consolo also makes an appearance, the author of *Lo spasimo di Palermo*, to whom I've never been able to put a face until now. And, hey, here's Sciascia walking through Córdoba and Seville!

'Come on sunshine, we've got to get on the road,' the others urge me.

BUT WHERE ARE WE GOING? Our time is short and we must also get to Messina before midnight. We could manage to visit one more town, always assuming we've got money left. Caltanissetta? No, it's famous for being the *ugly duckling* of the interior. What about Enna? The ancient Castrogiovanni, home to Proserpine, capital to the earth mother cult of Demeter, navel of Sicily, one of the island's high points at 930 metres.

'Snow chains obligatory', reads the traffic sign less than five kilometres from our destination. A snowfall won't be awaiting us, but certainly a very welcoming fresh breeze. We're in the colder part of Sicily, even though it's the month of July. Due to the altitude and location, very few visitors come here at this time of year. We've also noticed how much sparser the local population is than on the coast. According to statistics, only one in five Sicilians live in the interior.

In spite of this, I'm sure these inland areas are very much appreciated by the islanders, perhaps because they always offered a safe refuge. When the invaders arrived time and again by sea, the only way out left to the Sicilians was to take to the mountains. It is said that Sciascia, who studied in Caltanissetta and used to brag about never having swum in the sea, excused the thalassophobia of his compatriots in the following manner: 'This great Mediterranean island, its way of being, its life, seems to turn inward, clinging to the high plains and mountains, it tries to evade the sea and shut it out behind a curtain of heights and walls, to create the near perfect illusion that the sea doesn't exist (an idea not lacking metaphorical impact during the annual harvest) and that Sicily isn't an island. It's like burying one's head in the sand; not looking at the sea so that the sea doesn't look at us. But the sea does indeed watch us.'

They take it with them, I think to myself. They believe it's something from which you can flee, but they run away with the sea in their backpacks, with the sea in their shoes, with the sea flowing in their veins. These island people will take a great step forward when they realise that, if you can't beat it, it's far better to join it.

WE LEAN OUT over the viewing point to see the distant picturesque white walls of Calascibetta and the steep valley, striped by the streaky clouds hovering above it. Goethe, who is always a bit of a killjoy, didn't like this landscape at all. 'The beans were blossoming in the plains below, but who could enjoy the view!' he stated in his travelogue, in reference to a limestone hillside formed from fossilised marine deposits covered with fields of broad bean plants in flower. We do enjoy the sight, and Ka orders Faust's father to shut up by grabbing the book from my hands and closing it with a loud clap.

We go up to the Lombardia Castle, which is well suited to the terrain and still better preserved, finally reaching its splendid Pisana watchtower. Much to our relief, they don't even have a ticket office lying in wait. The large courtyards are a sign that normal life was established here by the government of the day, and most certainly there would have been more than one, each carrying a different flag. The solidity of the walls speaks volumes about a time when this town must have been an impregnable fortress. The privileged position, not only in terms of the defensive slope, also shows an extraordinary good taste for landscape.

We buy some snacks from a *pannineria*. We want to eat in the shade of a church, in one of the many squares breaking up the winding street plan of the town. But a one-eyed watchman, a revived but resentful Polyphemus, moves us on in a less than gracious manner, as if he's taken our galloping atheism for granted. We relocate a few metres away and demolish our *focaccia* and *arancini,* under a bronze statue, which someone identifies as Churchill but could be any old Napoleon. Iván has bought a bottle of *Ficodi*, a type of liqueur made from prickly pears, however, after our traumatic experience with *grappa* no one dares to give it much of a try. Properly fed, we return to Eureka.

THE ROADS MANAGE TO GIVE US one more fright. And it's all down to the popular belief, rigidly adhered to by Sicilians even when driving, that says if two can fit into the gap, so can three. The girls are sleeping in the back, but I spot out of the corner of my eye a car overtaking which is about to stop not only these pages seeing the light of day, but five of its principal characters – including our dear old Eureka – from participating in any further adventures. Iván, wiping his forehead, confirms this when he pulls in to a petrol station so we can have a break and calm our nerves.

'That overtaking manoeuvre. It was so close …' he tells me, cleaning the sweat from his brow.

The last moments in Messina are full of anxiety: pack the case as quickly as possible, return the exhausted Eureka, run to the railway station. I always hate leaving places I've visited, but this time I feel a much deeper anguish, a violent sensation of loss, a nostalgia already present before leaving, which still gives me butterflies as I write these lines. Messina, the plain, 'devastated Messina', on this night seems to be the most sadly beautiful city in the world.

The train arrives. I ask Ro not to stay and see us off, and we cling to each other in a long embrace. Someday I'll tell the story of the mix of conflicting emotions we experienced on our trip round Sicily. But that's for another book, not this one.

Don't look back I tell myself as I turn to push my luggage.

Rome, end of the line

DON'T LOOK BACK. And yet, when the train starts to shudder, the knot in my throat tightens further. We feel the train's carriages settling into the bowels of the ferry, how the temperature rises before we weigh anchor. Some travellers go up on deck. I stay seated here, in this compartment with its triple couchettes, rubbing my hands, with my head spinning, trying to control the strangely accelerated beat of my heart. Long minutes pass as we cross the Straits of Messina thus blindfolded. The boat's motors stop, we must already be in Reggio; we've reached the Italian peninsula, the carriages are readjusted on their rails and once again roll along terra firma.

To distract myself, I trace the route on the map by tracking the stations, I form the words as if they were dainty phonetic tidbits: Palmi, Gioia Tauro, Rosarno, Nicotera, Tropea, Vibo Marina, Pizzo, Eccellente, Lamezia, Amantea, Cosenza, Paola, Cetraro, Capo Bonifati, Sapri, Policastro, Bussentino, Vallo della Lucania, Castelnuovo, Agropoli Castellabate, Paestum, Battipaglia, Salerno …

I sleep fitfully. To avoid dying of heat and lack of oxygen we open the window, giving the atrocious engine noise free access to the compartment, which gets brutally amplified every time we go through one of the innumerable tunnels ahead of us. On the top bunk I think I hear Iván and Ka making love amid gasps and laughter. The promissory moon left behind in Messina is unrecognisable through the blurred glass. My strength sapped I don't see the sunrise.

'Ten minutes until we reach Rome!' calls out the ticket inspector just as I was starting to feel tired.

The others don't know the capital and our flight doesn't leave until early the following morning, so we spend the day visiting the well-known tourist spots. A breakfast of coffee and *cornetto* in the Termini café, exiting towards Santa Maria La Maggiore, we then walk around the Coliseum and the Forum, Agrippa's Pantheon with its marvellous dome, *disegno angelico e non umano*; the Trevi Fountain, the Spanish Steps, Piazza Venezia, the Campidoglio. We go down to the banks of the Tiber, back up to Sant' Angelo, and from there to the Vatican. They stop me from entering Saint Peter's in Bermudas, so I stay put taking notes among Bernini's columns. 'A paradise like the Vatican is my idea of hell', was Borges' observation of El Greco's paintings, with their christs guarded by bishops. I try to beat sleep by continuing to write.

Piazza Navona, the very expensive bar on the corner. The Campo dei Fiori, where Giordano Bruno was burnt by the Holy Inquisition. In a synagogue in the Jewish quarter they're celebrating a wedding. We skirt round the river and reach the Temple of Vesta, followed by Santa Maria, Ro's favourite church, with its proud bell tower scrapping the afternoon's clear blue sky, and then the *boca della verità* pardoning so many prying hands every day.

I've been following Borges, but he's also following me. Firstly, when we go around the Villa Borghese, which I blame for the Italian usage of *borgesiano* as the adjective describing things relating to the Argentinean, rather than the Spanish *borgiano*.* Then, I enter a Feltrinelli bookshop and see him in a large panel photograph, next to some other classic writers. Here you are again, maestro! I also discover among the shelves containing Scianna's books one full of short essays with, as far as I can discern, a none too shabby prose style,

---

* The common adjective for things relating to Borges in English is also Borgesian.

and another with old photos of Bagheria. However, my funds are almost spent and I can't allow myself any luxuries. I leave empty-handed.

The night at the airport is hellish. We hardly sleep a wink. The three of us bunched together on benches designed by one of the Marquis de Sade's better pupils, a sudden awful drop in temperature, a check-in time that never arrives. Almost two days without taking a shower, I feel terribly uncomfortable. Shifting around into impossible positions, pacing up and down the corridors, splashing water on my face from the washbasin in the toilets, smoking nervous cigarettes. At last the loudspeaker announces our imminent departure.

When we pass through the metal detectors, a security officer still tries to delay us further by asking for a minute set of nail clippers from Iván's case.

'Deadly weapons!' he exclaims in Italian as he blandishes them, gazing vacantly.

Time is a deadly weapon. Sleep is a deadly weapon. Memory is a deadly weapon.

The plane is already on the runway. We're going home.

~~~~

I know this image well. It was on the cover of a book of conversations between Borges and Osvaldo Ferrari, published in Spain by Emecé, which I've often looked at for my work. I've also seen it reproduced in many other places, making it one of the most well-known portraits of the writer.

A splendid profile of Borges. His white hair is a little unkempt, his brow silvered, the eyes rigid yet shining. And above his head, which is placed slightly to the fore, that cloud with its cotton borders lit by the sun, fraying in the ashen sky; as if it were a product of the maestro's thought, a foreboding of his, an emanation from his musings, or his frame of mind.

> Maybe a cloud is no less fixed
> than someone looking at it in the morning.

Selinunte, 1984

The cloud as container for an idea is a very old resource for the creators of short stories. Its tangible aspect has led to its portrayal as the customary bed for angels in classical art and as the pretext or object of more modern representations. Yet its ethereal, vaporous condition, added to its simple depiction, have also made the cumulus, stratus, cirrus and nimbus family a metaphor which never ages. That a photographer would dare to take this on in his work does seem a novel idea. That Borges was the one called on to collaborate in the experiment may not be totally arbitrary.

The cloud, '*the unmemorable cloud*' of his paradoxically unforgettable poems:

> ... Your mirrored face
> already is another face that blinked
> in day, our dubious labyrinth of space.
> We are the ones who leave. The multiple
> cloudbank dissolving in the dropping sun
> draws images of us. Ceaselessly will
> the rose become another rose. You are
> the cloud, the sea, you are oblivion,
> and you are whom you've lost, now very far.

I'm the one who leaves. And I'm also whom I've lost.

I'd like to think a cloud could also be a model for our dreams, for utopias, for all those unreachable things that still appear before our stunned eyes and make us take off in their pursuit. They could be rosy, like the sugary clouds of candy floss sold at fairs, or of a compact greyness like the one in the photograph. But we certainly won't rest until we discover them, trap them, make them our own, name them, pin them like butterflies into our own personal firmament. And if we never get the opportunity to possess them, it will be the search that acts as the greatest substitute for such happiness, the best consolation for our empty hands.

We often play at recognising familiar shapes in the clouds.

However, I remember Pep Quetglas, a Spanish architect who thinks and writes very well, tipped this game on its head in one of his essays. Instead of thinking about what a cloud looks like, he proposed that we ask ourselves what is cloud-like in our surroundings. I peer out of the little aeroplane window – clouds, clouds and dreams – and I delight in contemplating 'the sublime normality of the skies' as Lampedusa would have said. I then look back over the little red book. I'm pleased to have located all the places visited by Borges during his trip around Sicily, but I know I'm missing one. This one. As a good collector, the outstanding task, the absent card in my album, won't let me feel satisfied.

I have to find that cloud. Out there somewhere.

Palermo, Buenos Aires

A YEAR OR so has passed since I was in Palermo, the capital of my terrible, yet beloved stone raft, now I'm in the other Palermo, the district of Buenos Aires, founded in the seventeenth century by a certain Giovanni Palermo, a Sicilian farmer. There will be those who think I've travelled a considerable distance. But, in some ways, I feel I'm in the same place, that I've just been going round in circles for all this time, that I still haven't left the island. Time and again I've returned thanks to books, music, cinema, photographs. I haven't stopped visiting it.

The summer can also be cold. Here, in Buenos Aires, buttoned up to the eyeballs, I've recognised the distant cousins of the archetypical Borgesian tiger among the cats of the Botanical Garden, I've winked at beautiful statues, I've bought trinkets from the street stalls and strolled through the rose gardens. Gone is the fig tree shading the garden wall, as is the stubborn little brook and the peanut seller's bugle, which Borges found so very touching as he used to listen from his home in block 2100, Calle Serrano. I've held the lacquer cane belonging to the maestro, I've leafed through the three small volumes of the *Divine Comedy* he used to read on buses, three small shrines upholstered in blue leather, home to a harsh onslaught of dioptres.

I've sensed the living presence of Borges in the streets of

this town. And that of Sicily, of Italy as a whole, reflected in much of the architecture, in the accomplishments of the better pizzerias such as Guerrín and Los Inmortales, in certain of the Saracen faces crossing the roads and in certain flavours of the local music. And, of course, in the surnames: Baiardino, Pisavini, Mastronardi, Decotte, Calandrelli, Barbieri, Fatone, Ferrari, Mezzera, Dell'Oro, Barletta, Fioravanti, Loneri, Sicardi, Calvetti, Bianchi, Rossi, Lanteri, Muzzio, Pezzoni, Sussini, and so many others invading the city's corpulent telephone book, its letter boxes, shop signs and newspaper headlines.

My essay on Borges was published and I was lucky enough to be given the daring opportunity of presenting it here, right here in the Mecca for Borgiophiles, in the homeland and backyard of the maestro. It's a bad time for Buenos Aires. It's no longer a place full of cut-throats and lowlife who perhaps only live on through literature, but of friendly people weathering the storm of the economic crisis, fighting for their daily bread without denying a smile to the dauntless Spaniard, recently arrived and keen to devour everything with his eyes.

I go into a bookshop and it's not long before I come across his *Aleph*, his *Fictions*, his *Brodie's Report*. Tempted to open them at random, I feel my hands tremble like an alcoholic before a glass of gin or a compulsive gambler in front of a casino. I made a promise to my friends, and I'm going to keep it. Then my gaze falls on a title that grabs my attention: *Amores Sicilianos.* I pick it up and start to leaf through it straight away. It's by an Argentinean writer, Vlady Kociancich, who tells the story of her journey from Buenos Aires to Palermo: leaving aside the difference in dates, her flight crosses paths with my own. I look at the image on the sleeve. She's an attractive older woman, with straight black hair, light-coloured eyes and a cold smile. She seems familiar ... Of course, why didn't I remember before! Vlady, I have a photograph of her with Borges. If memory serves me, she was reading him something about Anglo-Saxon literature.

She had shorter curly hair, a rounder face, but it's definitely her. How many people in the world can be Argentinean and called Vlady Kociancich?

I leave the Borgesian volumes where they are, if for no other reason than the fact I've got them at home, and I go to the checkout with the book by the lady from Buenos Aires. I have a feeling that the circle may be closing as I do this. Didn't Spinoza say that a passion can only be tamed by another stronger one? Borges by Sicily: I smile as I imagine what new journey I'll have to invent in order to escape from this new snare.

But it has come to an end, truly. The damage is done, I presented my book and now it no longer belongs to me. I did what I could as it was an honourable text and I feel I kept my promise to the Argentinean. It reminds me of an anecdote from my illustrious countryman, the great Fernando Quiñones, who fearing the Borgesian influence was affecting his writing too much, bravely fought to free himself from it. One fine day, he was eventually able to declare: 'Maestro, it has cost me a lot, but I'll now really be free of you, finally I'll be free from Borges.' The man himself shook his head melancholically and retorted: 'What luck, I still haven't managed it yet.'

In this other Palermo, the Palermo of Evaristo Carriego, among these 'corners of aggression or loneliness', I came to put an end to my journey. And I'm here to express my utmost emotional gratitude to the companion who has been with me throughout so many kilometres. To my infallible friend, to my old immortal master, to my blind guide.

I'm referring, as you'll have already guessed, to love.

Cádiz, July 2003 – Buenos Aires, July 2004.

Epilogue

A<small>LMOST TEN YEARS</small> have passed since *Viaje a la Sicilia con un guía ciego* saw the light of day, and to return to these pages makes me feel a mixture of discomfort and relief. Discomfort, because only at that age could one allow oneself the nerve to write about such a rich location with such a fledgling knowledge, something which today, no doubt, I wouldn't dare to do; and relief on realising that the book, with all its naivety and audacity, is still readable and will provide, I hope, a certain enjoyment. I know for a fact, furthermore, that the book has accompanied many visitors to the island, as many friends as those unknown to me, and this type of stowaway travel tucked into someone else's luggage is a pleasure that I couldn't and wouldn't want to deny.

Certainly there are many details which, today, from my perspective, with far greater experience, I would like to change or qualify. I don't want to do it though, because I feel that my outlook then, although ingenuous in many ways, shouldn't be adulterated. However, I can't leave unrecognised the book's biggest mistake in appreciation, specifically the chapter in which I consider the idea that Sicily is an island almost without music. The discovery during subsequent years of the Mancuso brothers, Etta Scollo, Marian Trapassi, Carmen Consoli, the percussionist Alfio Antico or the saxophonist Francesco Cafiso, let alone the legendary Rosa Balistreri, piques my guilty conscience every time I look through that section. Let's hope this apology serves to wash away such notions.

These days, the life of books is evermore limited, their renumeration evermore meagre, therefore the best one can ask of them is that they foster lasting friendships and collaborations. Among those I would like to mention in print, hoping not to have committed any serious omissions, are the names of Ferdinando Scianna, the Sciascia family, Gioacchino and Nicoletta Lanza Tommasi, Georges Salameh and family, Letizia Battaglia, Sara Anselmi, Antonio Battaglia, Roberto Alajmo, Giacomo Cacciatore, Giuseppe Schillaci, Natale Tedesco, Dina Trapassi, Miguel Ángel Cuevas and, of course, my dear Suzanne and Andy Edwards, the latter of whom translated this journey.

I often return to Sicily and each time I go back I discover a new treasure, a marvel that was hitherto unknown to me. I am, therefore, in a position to confirm that the island, with its wonders and its dramas, is inexhaustible. This journey couldn't, then, give the last word in any respect, but it aspires, at most, to be an invitation to continue exploring – to take up the discovery of the island at the point where others have stopped.

Acknowledgements

During my *viaggio* I incurred many a well-founded debt. The first is to Ferdinando Scianna, the prodigious polyphemus from Bagheria. In addition, I must also share my Sicilian affections among Doctor Natale Tedesco, the painter Gianni Allegra, professor Dina Trapassi and her husband, Javier.

On the Borgesian side of things, I would like to thank María Kodama for the kindness she has shown me on the fleeting occasions we have met in Cádiz and Seville. Maximum gratitude also to the adorable Irma Zangara, my hostess at the Fundación Borges, likewise for the Buenos Aires hospitality of Abelardo Castillo, Sylvia Iparraguirre, Daniel Divinski and José Carlos Gallardo.

Thanks also to Ilya U. Topper, Kamala Orozo and Rocío Lesmes, for their blessed patience; to César Cabanas, Mar Barbero, Olivia Pierrugues, Edmundo Desnoes, Pisco Lira, Antonio Acedo, María José Ramírez and Nacho Garmendia, for their loyal complicity; to Antonio Rivero Taravillo, David González Romero, Sergio Rojas-Marcos, Pepe Arévalo and Manuel Pimentel, for the warmth they have given to these pages. And to Ángela Cañal, who carried the first manuscript on the plane and who carries on dealing with my sleepless nights on terra firma.

Bibliography

Agnello Horby, Simonetta. *The Almond Picker*. Penguin,
   2006.

Ali, Tariq. *A Sultan in Palermo*. Verso, 2006.

Andó, Roberto. *Diario senza date*. Gea Schirò, 2008.

Argullol, Rafael. *Lampedusa*. Destino, 1990.

Borges, Jorge Luis. *Labyrinths*. Penguin Classics, 2000.
   Selected Poems 1926 –1967. Penguin, 1985.
   Selected Poems. Penguin, 2000.
   Atlas. Viking, 1986.

Brancati, Vitaliano. *Don Giovanni in Sicily*. Troubador,
   2009.

Bufalino, Gesualdo. *A Plague-spreader's Tale*. Harvill, 1999.
   Blind Argus. Harvil, 1992.
   L'uomo invaso. Bompiani, 2014.
   Night's Lies. Harvill, 1999.
   Qui pro quo. Bompiani, 2014.
   Calende greche. Bompiani, 2014.
   Tommaso and the Blind Photographer. Harvill, 2000.

Buzzati, Dino. *The Bear's Famous Invasion of Sicily*. Harper
   Collins, 2005.

Calvino, Italo. *Invisible Cities*. Harvest Books, 1978.

Camilleri, Andrea. *Un mese con Montalbano*. Mondadori,
   2010.
   La ópera de Vigàta. Destino, 2000.
   Excursion to Tindari. Picador, 2006.
   The Voice of the Violin. Picador, 2005.

The Terracotta Dog. Picador, 2004.

The Shape of Water. Picador, 2003.

The Scent of the Night. Picador, 2007.

Rounding the Mark. Picador, 2007.

Privo di titolo. Sellerio, 2012.

Campbell, Federico. *La memoria de Sciascia.* Fondo de Cultura Económica, 2004.

Collura, Matteo. *Il maestro di Regalpetra. Vita di Leonardo Sciascia.* Tea, 2007.

Consolo, Vincenzo. *The Smile of the Unknown Mariner.* Carcanet, 1994.

Lo spasimo di Palermo. Mondadori, 1999.

Durrell, Lawrence. *Sicilian Carousel.* Viking, 1977.

Fernández, Dominique. *La zattere della Gorgona.* Sellerio, 1992.

Fest, Joachim. *A contraluz. Viaje por Italia.* Galaxia Gutenberg, 1997.

Goethe, Johann W. *Italian Journey.* Penguin Classics, 1970.

Grasa, Ismael. *Sicilia.* El Cobre, 2004.

Kermoal, Jacques and Bartolomei, Martine. *La mafia se sienta a la mesa.* Tusquets, 1998.

Kociancich, Vlady. *Amores sicilianos.* Seix Barral, 2004.

Lanzafame, Giovanni. *Caminando por la tierra de María,* Almuzara, 2005.

Luque de Diego, Alejandro. *Palabras Mayores. Borges/ Quiñones, 25 años de amistad.* Ayuntamiento de Cádiz, 2004.

Mansilla, Luis M. *Apuntes de viaje al interior del tiempo.* Fundación Caja de Arquitectos, 2002.

Maupassant, Guy de. *Sicily.* Italica Press, 2007.

Messina, María de. *Behind Closed Doors: Her Father's House and Other Stories of Sicily.* Feminist Press, 2007.

House in the Shadows. Marlboro, 1991.

Orlando, Francesco. *Ricordo di Lampedusa.* Bollati Boringhieri, 1996.

P., Melissa. *One Hundred Strokes of the Brush Before Bed.* Serpent's Tail, 2004.

Pirandello, Luigi. *The Late Mattia Pascal.* Dedalus, 1988.
Six Characters in Search of an Author. Nick Hern Books, 2003.
The Turn. Hesperus, 2007.
Naked Masks (Liolà). Penguin, 1957.
One, No One and One Hundred Thousand. Marsillo, 1992.
Tales of Madness: Selection from Pirandello's "Short Stories for a Year". Branden, 1984.
Tales of Suicide: Selection from Pirandello's "Short Stories for a Year". Branden, 1988.

Puzo, Mario. *The Godfather.* Arrow Books, 2009.
The Fortunate Pilgrim. Arrow Books, 1992.

Quinel, C. and De Montgon, A. *Cuentos y leyendas de Sicilia.* Romerman Ed., 1963.

Reyero, Miguel. *Sicilia.* Laertes, 1997.

Robb, Peter. *Midnight in Sicily.* Harvill, 1999.

Roberto, Federico De. *The Viceroys.* MacGibbon & Kee, 1962.

Saint Phalle, Natalie de. *Hoteles literarios.* Alfaguara, 1993.

Sanmarco, Carmelo. *Cocinar a la siciliana.* Arnone Ed., 1998.

Sapienza, Goliarda. *The Art of Joy.* Penguin, 2013.

Savatteri, Gaetano. *I siciliani.* Laterza, 2006.

Schiller, Friedrich von. *The Bride of Messina.* Kessinger 2004.

Scianna, Ferdinando. *Quelli di Bagheria.* Peliti, 2003
Jorge Borges photographié par Ferdinando Scianna. Franco Sciardelli, 1999.

Sciascia, Leonardo. *The Day of the Owl.* Granta Books, 2014.
To Each His Own. Carcanet, 1992.
Candido: A Dream Dreamed in Sicily. Harvill, 1995.
Ore di Spagna. Pungitopo, 1988.

Il contesto. Adelphi, 1997.

One Way or Another. Paladin, 1989.

Dalle parti degli infedeli. Adelphi, 2002.

The Council of Egypt. Carcanet, 1999.

Nero su nero. Adelphi, 1991.

Il teatro della memoria. Einaudi, 1981.

Mata-Hari en Palermo. Montesinos, 1986.

Sin esperanza no pueden plantarse olivos. Laia, 1987.

1912+1. Carcanet, 1989.

Open Doors and Three Novellas. Vintage Books, 1994.

The Knight and Death and Other Stories. Carcanet, 1991.

Alfabeto pirandelliano. Adelphi, 1989.

La sentenza memorabile. Sellerio, 1982.

The Wine Dark Sea. Granta Books, 2014.

Salt in the Wound followed by The Death of the Inquisitor. Orion, 1969.

The Death of an Inquisitor and Other Stories (Little Chronicles/The Captain and the Witch). Carcanet, 1990.

Cruciverba. Adelphi, 2000.

A Simple Story. Hesperus, 2009.

Fatti diversi di storia letteraria e civile. Adelphi, 2009.

Sicilian Uncles. Granta Books, 2014.

The Moro Affair and the Mystery of Majorana. New York review of Books, 2004.

L'onorevole – Recitazione della controversia liparitana dedicata ad A. D. – I mafiosi. Adelphi, 1995.

L'adorabile Stendhal. Adelphi, 2003.

I pugnalatori. Einaudi, 1976.

Titote, Virgilio. *Viejas y nuevas historias de Sicilia.* Fundamentos, 1989.

Tomasi di Lampedusa, Giuseppe. *The Leopard.* Collins and Harvill, 1960.

Verdura, Fulco di. *Happy Summer Days.* Phoenix, 2000.

Verga, Giovanni. *I Malavoglia (The House by the Medlar Tree).* Dedalus, 2008

Mastro Don Gesualdo. Greenwood, 1976.

Vittorini, Elio. *Women of Messina*. New Directions, 1973.

    Le città del mondo. Biblioteca Univ. Rizzoli, 2012.

    Dark and the Light: Erica and La Garibaldina, Two Short Novels. Greenwood, 1977.

    In Sicily and The Twilight of the Elephant. W W Norton, 1974.

    Conversations in Sicily. Canongate Books, 2004.

VV.AA. *Ore di Sciascia*. Revista Caleta, no. 12. Cádiz, 2006.

VV.AA. *Gli anni di Sciascia e Bufalino*. Gruppo Editoriale Kalos, 2001.

Quasimodo, Salvatore. *Selected Poems*. Penguin Modern European Poets, 1965.

Zagajewski, Adam. *Eternal Enemies*. Farrar, Straus & Giroux, 2009.